Grandfather Navelle and son Edward

LIVING CREOLE AND SPEAKING IT FLUENTLY

VIVIAN MALVEAUX

authorHOUSE®

AuthorHouse™
1663 Liberty Drive
Bloomington, IN 47403
www.authorhouse.com
Phone: 1-800-839-8640

© 2009 Vivian Malveaux. All rights reserved.

No part of this book may be reproduced, stored in a retrieval system, or transmitted by any means without the written permission of the author.

First published by AuthorHouse 6/30/2009

ISBN: 978-1-4389-7339-5 (sc)

Printed in the United States of America
Bloomington, Indiana

This book is printed on acid-free paper.

IN MEMORY

In loving memory of Neville, Modeste and all our deceased ancestors of the Briscoe Family. You will always be in our hearts and in our prayers. We are forever grateful for our heritage.

My oldest brother, Junior

My fourth brother, Merrick

My fifth (youngest) brother, Michael

DEDICATION

To my three brothers:
Merrick, Michael, and Junior Briscoe,
Three of the nicest, sweetest guys I have ever known.
Qui j'ame ton.

TABLE OF CONTENTS

In Memory	v
Dedication	ix
Foreword	xiii
Acknowledgments	xv
Family Prayer	xvii
Important dates in the founding of Louisiana and New Orleans	xix
Introduction	1
A Creole Story and Dictionary	5
Losing Mama	12
Brother Joel	39
Religion	42
Le Creole	49
The Dictionary	70

FOREWORD

Language holds the key to understanding who we are because it tells us how we think… about ourselves, about the world around us, and about how we relate to each other. Because our ways of thinking change over time, so too does language change. Some languages change dramatically or disappear altogether as the speakers change their habits, and generations of speakers die out, taking their language with them.

When languages die out or disappear, it is a sad event because we lose an important part of human culture and history. Creole is a language that is on the "endangered list" and here, Vivian Malveaux has tried to preserve the language and history of Creole and its speakers. I have known Vivian as a neighbor and a dear friend, and I have enormous respect for her work and dedication to this book. Vivian overcame tremendous obstacles in her life, and has produced here a remarkable book—remarkable in that it not only describes important Creole words, but also preserves the flavor and cadence of Creole… then and now. What Vivian has written is an important document that preserves a disappearing language and recalls and describes a significant part of

Vivian Malveaux

American history. That this history is both a collective history of the Creole-speaking people of the United States and a highly singular and personal history is further testimony to its significance.

Carol Helstosky
Department of History
University of Denver

ACKNOWLEDGMENTS

I am deeply grateful to the following: to Mary Gehman who I cannot thank enough. Without her this book would not exist. To all of the people who helped, my children Mary Catherine and Stanley Paul.

Thanks to Carol Helstosky and Martin Gloege, who were there for me from beginning to end.

I am ever so grateful to Tom and Jo Roberts who helped put my CD together.

Thanks to Karen and Bill Krenshaw for their help.

Wayman Carter the computer expert, thank you. Thanks to Hugh Robertson, Linda Trazna, Dan Willgang. All of my family from whom I gathered information, pictures, and encouragement. Charles and Janis Pete, Virginia and Linda Jolivette, Joseph and Gladys Broussard, Beatrice and Ann Marie Richard, and my cousins Bernice Rideaux, and Betty Briscoe, you all had a hand in this and I thank you all more than I can express.

Merci beaucou.
Vivian Malveaux

Vivian Malveaux

> *"But as for you,*
> *be strong and do not give up,*
> *for your work will be rewarded."*
> 2 Chronicles 15:7

CREATIVITY

The truly creative mind in any field is no more than this: a human creature born abnormally, inhumanly sensitive. To them a touch is a blow, a sound is a noise, misfortune is a tragedy, a joy is an ecstasy, a friend is a lover, a lover is a God and failure is death.

Add to this cruelly delicate organism the overpowering necessity to create, create, create so that without the creating of music or poetry or books or buildings, or something of meaning, his very breath is cut off from him. They must create, must pour out creation. By some strange, unknown, inward urgency he is not really alive unless he is creating.

Pearl S. Buck

FAMILY PRAYER

Loving God,
    we ask you to bless our family
    and the life we share together.
Help us to work with one another,
    sharing our gifts and talents
    to make our family grow in faith, love, and service.
Help us to stay together joyfully,
    giving of our time and of ourselves
    to make our family happy.
Help us to love one another
    and always be eager to show that love.
In joys and in sorrows,
    In good times and bad,
    may we give strength to one another.
As we strive to follow the example of Jesus, Mary and Joseph,
    may we respect every one's human dignity
    in all our daily relationships.
Finally, may we all one day share together
    in the everlasting happiness of your heavenly family.
Amen.

Vivian Malveaux

IMPORTANT DATES IN THE FOUNDING OF LOUISIANA AND NEW ORLEANS[1]

1699............The founding of Louisiana as a French colony.

1717-31........The Company of the Indies contracted by John Law to populate Louisiana.

1718............The city of New Orleans was founded.

1719............The first cargo of slaves was brought to Louisiana to save the struggling French colony. Two thousand, eighty three slaves were imported.

1722............The capital of Louisiana moves from Mobile to New Orleans.

1722............For the first time records were kept of blacks in New Orleans.

1724............The Black Code was established to give rights to slaves and free blacks.

---

1   For a more complete timeline of Louisiana's French history, see the website for CODOFIL (Conseil pour la développement du français en Louisiane), http://www.codofil.org/english/lafrenchhistory.html .

1724............The first record of a free black lawsuit in court.

1725............First free black marriages in church.

1730............The Company of the Indies goes bankrupt and Louisiana reverts to French ownership.

1733............The earliest record of slaves freed in Louisiana.

1740s...........The slave trade direct from Africa almost closed.

1751............African market was established by slaves in *Place des Negres* at what is Congo Square today.

1751............Police code issued regarding behavior of blacks.

1754-63.........Seven years war in Europe and trade with France is halted.

1760............The King's slaves in Louisiana are sold, which leads to the end of the slave force.

1762............Louisiana is transferred from French to Spanish rule.

The Spanish Period, 1763-1802

1763............Louisiana transferred from France to Spain.

1764............First slave patrol organized to round up runaways slaves.

1769............Spanish rule finally established, minor changes took place in the Black Code.

1770............A large number of free women of color acquired real estate in the city.

Living Creole and Speaking it Fluently

1771............Lebreton, a Carrollton planter, was killed by his personal slaves who are then killed.

1778............Acadians and Islenos begin settling southern Louisiana.

1788-94........Two great fires destroy most of original city of New Orleans. Blacks do most of the rebuilding.

1789-95........The French Revolution: all slaves in French West Indies are set free.

1795............Pointe Coupee Uprising: slaves and free blacks unite and march on New Orleans but were stopped by the militia.

1796............A ban on all blacks entering Louisiana. The Black Code was made more restrictive for slaves and free blacks.

1802............Spain goes nearly bankrupt and Louisiana returns to French rule.

INTRODUCTION

As a native of Louisiana growing up Creole, I feel compelled to write about my life and culture. Raised without a Mother or a Father most of the time, I was fortunate enough to have family, including a loving Grandmother, to care for me until I got married. Of course it wasn't always perfect, but they taught me enough to lead a respectable and fulfilling life.

I did not know that I was Creole until I became a teenager. My Grandmother always spoke Creole to me and I would answer in English; she did not approve. As I got older I learned to appreciate the fact that I knew a second language. In her honor I am including a Creole Dictionary and I hope she knows that I did. Also, I have done this because Creole is said to be a dying language. I hope others can learn with this easy to learn Dictionary and accompanying CD.

My primary objective for writing this book is for the preservation of Creole culture and language, which has long been ignored and rarely acknowledged in spite of its uniqueness. *"There is no state in the union, hardly any spot of like size on the globe where the man of color has lived so intensely, made so much progress, been of such historical importance (as in Louisiana) and yet about so little is known."* (Alice Dunbar Nelson).

In spite of much literature written on the subject, many are unaware of the contributions that the Creoles made to New Orleans and the State of Louisiana. Because of ethnic bias, the history and culture of Creoles have been ignored by mainstream America. The word "Creole" was first used by French and Spanish settlers who arrived in Louisiana; they referred to their children as Creoles because they were born in a new land of mixed culture. The faces of Creoles have features and skin tones that show centuries of inter-racial mixing of African, Indian, Latin and European.

After the Haitian revolt, some of the Haitian Creoles were brought to New Orleans along with slaves to work in the cane and cotton fields. The history of the slaves is well known. But in the shadow of this history are the free people of color, as the French named them. After the Civil War, they were called Creoles of Color, and later this was shortened to Creoles. Many free men of color joined the Battle of New Orleans, others joined the side of the Confederacy in the Civil War. Free women of color were nurses, hairdressers and dressmakers to upper-class French women. The husbands, sons, and brothers of these upper-class French women sometimes had a hidden family among the free women of color and set them up in small houses and had children with them, giving their natural offspring their own French last names and passing on to them their property and wealth.

New Orleans had the largest community of Creoles in the United States. There they developed their own leaders who helped shaped the state of Louisiana. In every change of government the Creoles used their influence and are credited with helping to shape policies in Washington D.C. on civil rights and suffrage for blacks. In 1719 the first ship of slaves were brought to New Orleans and their hard work saved the struggling French Community. Recently a woman from New York wrote that she does not believe that Creoles really exist.

Cajuns were exiled from Nova Scotia by the British Government, and many of them settled in South Louisiana and have shared the French, Catholic heritage with Creoles. They speak different French dialects. Ironically, both Cajun and Creole languages are on the endangered list, since the older Generations are passing away. The younger generation seems to have ignored that part of their culture in order to fit in with the mainstream.

Many Creoles have left Louisiana, and now reside in other parts of the country seeking better jobs and to escape segregation in the south. An estimated 15,000 Creoles live in Los Angeles alone, while others moved to Chicago, Detroit, Houston and other parts of the United States and Mexico.

In 2005, it seems that hurricane Katrina was determined to destroy everything in its path, in New Orleans and other cities along the gulf, leaving people stranded and homeless in the aftermath. Some could do nothing but leave New Orleans and other parts of the country, going where ever they could find shelter, even if it was only temporary. Others were afraid to return to the crime-ridden city, fearful that another hurricane could strike again.

Every time Creoles move away from Louisiana, they lose a part of their culture, unless they maintain contact through festivals and membership clubs such as Colorado Friends of Cajun and Zydeco Music and Dance in Denver, Colorado and in other parts of the country. With music provided by the hot Zydeco and Cajun bands that travel all over the country and parts of Europe and the Orient, I sincerely believe that, even though the language dies, Creole culture will survive.

A CREOLE STORY AND DICTIONARY

In September of 2005, the organization *Alliance Française of Denver* held a program called "Language Preservation." Since I am a native of Louisiana now residing in Denver, I was asked to give a presentation on the subject of the dying language of Creole. When the presentation was over, the audience was very interested; they asked questions and said that it was a beautiful language that should be preserved along with the Creole culture.

I told them what it was like growing up Creole, living on a farm in Opelousas, Louisiana where the population at that time was around ten thousand. Opelousas is about 200 miles west of New Orleans in St. Landry Parish (Louisiana has parishes rather than counties, as in France) which became the largest parish in the state. It is the third oldest city in Louisiana.

European traders were the first to enter the territory of the Opelousas Indians. The city was named the parish seat and records indicate that the first courthouse was constructed in 1806 on a square in the middle of town. Since that time, four other structures have been built on the same spot, and the present courthouse was built in 1939.

Louisiana was admitted to the union in 1821. During the Civil War, Opelousas became the state capital for nine months in 1862, after Baton Rouge fell under Union control. The former Lieutenant Governor at that time was Homere Mouton, whose house became the Governor's mansion, a title that it still bears. The main street that runs in front of the courthouse in Opelousas is called Landry Street. It was where my family took care of business about property and taxes and so forth, and once in a while I was allowed to tag along with one of the adults when they went shopping. At the time I thought that it was a very large place. It was the center of my world, away from the farm. At ten years old, I loved walking along the streets where the old trees were so large that their roots raised the sidewalk, like little hills. I liked the quietness when there weren't so many cars on the street.

I remember looking at all of the beautiful things in the showcases of the stores, even though we weren't able to purchase any of it. At Christmas time, when the city was all lit up, the thought occurred to my childish mind, that maybe I could get something for Christmas from Abdellas, the largest department store in town on Main Street.

There was only one signal light in town. At rush hour there were probably three cars at the red light. I still love my home town, but it's really my family that I love and miss the most. Of course there were no phones at that time, so when we saw dust rising on that lone dusty road in front of our house, we knew that "somebody was coming." There's a Briscoe (my family name), road on the way to my house, so on Sundays I could sit on the sofa facing the road, listening to the Lafayette Playboys on the radio and I knew that my date was on the way, by a cloud of dust rising. These days the roads are graveled.

We had a neighbor who lived in the house just before ours and she watched as he got near and stopped, got out of the car and dust off his clothes before he arrived.

My sister Madelle and her husband Rudolph owned the property where we lived so we worked sun up to sun down, either to plant the crops or harvest them. Like all farmers, we were at the mercy of Mother Nature. Sometimes, even though I was very young, I could tell when it was a bad crop by the look on their faces or the sound of their voice when they talked about it.

We lived in an old house that had a Garson-ire (stairs that go to second story from the porch) which was where the boys slept and this space was off limits to the girls.

We raised most of our food, including vegetables, sweet potatoes and corn. We also grew cotton. We worked hard, but we had some good times too. We never missed Mass on Sundays and Holidays. When we left, we just pulled the door closed. We had no locks. I guess we didn't have anything that anyone wanted.

We had Mardi Gras, which means Fat Tuesday, when most people stuffed themselves with food before Lent begins (as if it could last until Easter). Mardi Gras is the day before Lent begins, which is also when Catholics fast on Fridays and certain days before Easter Sunday. In my neighborhood, my brothers made their own costumes for Mardi Gras and rode around in wagons, on horse back (or what ever was available) to take them from house to house, in the community to ask for a chicken, or any ingredients that could be used to make gumbo at the end of the day. The costumes were so scary and strange, the young children hid behind their mother's skirts, while peeping out to see what was going on. There was no eating meat on Fridays or Wednesdays (I think the Catholic Church threw in Wednesdays just for good measure), dancing was definitely out and so was having any kind of good enjoyable fun until after Easter Sunday. We didn't even listen to music on the radio during Lent. I couldn't wait for it to be over.

My sister Madelle was a strong Christian disciplinarian, who did not put up with children talking back and disobeying the rules. She raised nine children of her own and some of her brothers and sisters, myself included. I still have a strong image of her sitting and having her young children kneeling beside her saying prayers, sometimes they were too young to pronounce the prayer words correctly, but even at that age they knew they had to say prayers every night. Some nights we tried to say prayers together, but the older members fell asleep from exhaustion, after working hard all day.

Madelle and her husband called each other "*neg*", which to them was a term of endearment. We've heard some of the Cajuns call their children *neg*, which is French for the "N-word" we wondered if they knew what they were saying. I walked to school, about a mile one way, when I didn't have to work in the fields.

I had always been an overly sensitive, shy and lonely child. I was skinny and I must admit not very attractive. So at school I was taken advantage of and often bullied. Other girls my age were attractive and well built. They played sports and games, never asking me to join in, so the only thing left for me to do was go to the library and read. I became so good at it I was valedictorian of my class, in eighth grade. I was so timid that I felt faint to stand in front of the class to speak.

The girls in my class would ask me to write love letters to the guys they were interested in. So I'd write the letter, and they'd say "that's exactly what I wanted to say!"

There were other Creoles at the school that I attended, but most of my friends were not Creole. As it were, I was put down because of skin color (and the fact that I spoke Creole).

Among my immediate family and acquaintances were French names such as: Lagers (pronounced Lachea), Babineaux, Malveaux, Thibodeaux,

Fonteneaux, Richards and Gillouries. My father's surname is Briscoe (Irish, like the potato) who married my Mother Beatrice Broussard.

Do not believe the stories about cousins marrying, at least not in my family. When a couple decided to get married, one of the first questions the parents asked were, "Who's you Mama and Daddy chere? And where you'll gon' live?" (Probably to make sure it wasn't with them). Most importantly, to make sure they weren't related, "we got to check on that marry-ing" and believe me, the two families got together and discussed this thing to find out if Taunt Na-Na, "is dat the one dat use to stay on dat old no count SOB's place… dat was so mean to black people… she was married to Unc Jacq?" "Maen, if das the one, they kin ya!" "Maen, das how com they lak each other so much…but if they terd cousins, is ok if they marry and we pray the chirin come out ok."

But sometimes they say, "ah non chere, das too close." Then there was a lot of boohoo-ing and "if das the case I'll never get married if I can't have her." But you know "by that next yer, he done find somebody else to marry yea. And das why day took you to different dances, so you can meet somebody without dem French nam. And they check dat out befo dat get too serious too."

I don't think that it's generally known that only 6 states allow first cousins to marry, because of the potential damage to future children. All 50 states allow second cousins to marry. I certainly am not advocating cousins marry each other, but I mention it only because, there is a stigma attached to cousin couples.

My parents Felix and Beatrice

LOSING MAMA

My Mother Beatrice died when I was four years old. At the wake I remember that all of the people were crying as I lay my head on my Grandma's lap, but I didn't know what had happened, I cried because every one else cried. I am sure they told me but I didn't understand that it meant my Mom was gone forever. Having been only four when she died, the only information I have about her is what I've learned from others.

I've heard that people get premonitions before they die. My oldest brother breaks down and sobs each time he tells about when Mom was leaving for the hospital, she asked that he help take care of the younger children, because she didn't think she would return home. I still get a heart ache each time I look at her death certificate. After I grew older and started having friends, I developed a shyness that I didn't over come until I got married. I didn't realize how much I missed her until my friends talked about their Mothers.

I've been told that when Mom was alive, she gave food to indigent people who walked around in the area where we lived, (they were called hobos) even though we didn't have that much to share and my Dad didn't approve. Once as she was riding along in a buggy, when she was forced off the road and found lying in a ditch, still holding her young baby in her arms, I was the baby. I have heard several people say that she was a good person. She died in childbirth, having too many babies too soon and probably not having the proper care in the hospital.

There were eleven children in my family. Madelle was the oldest, then Edith, Jeneva, Junior, Eunice, Joel, Vivian, Sidney and Merrick. When Mother died, Dad remarried and they had Hilda Ann and Michael. After my Mom died, Merrick was adopted by an uncle and his wife. Sidney joined the Marines when he was old enough.

MY FATHER

My father Felix became depressed and distant after Mom died, but before moving to Beaumont, Texas he became closer to his youngest children and tried to entertain them by playing his accordion and encouraging us to dance, and sometimes he would do a dance that he called the choo-choo train by moving his feet back and fourth and ending by kicking one foot in the air and then try to convince us to imitate his dance.

When he drank coffee in the morning, we always wanted some of his, so he took another coffee pot and made some for us, but it was mostly milk and he called it café o lai, he actually brought cups of it to the bed for each of us.

Later when he moved to Texas I would go visit during the summer. When I was there he loved to play jokes on me or who ever was available. If I was reading a book he would pass by a light switch and turn it off, to get my attention, and then walk away with a smile. His wife Hilma was the victim of his jokes many times. He loved to listen to baseball games on the radio. And during a break he would say to his wife "Hilma don't you care that my team is losing"? Invariably she always answered no, but he never missed a chance to harass her and she enjoyed it. Dad wasn't very talkative but he loved to tease.

One of the first jobs my Father had was at a Priest Seminary in Louisiana which is how he learned to read a little. I was always proud to see him trying to read the news paper, but I wondered how much he understood. Whenever I went to visit, after hugs and kisses, he always asked "did you missed me" then insisted on giving me money for paper and stamps so I could stay in touch.

Once when I was about eight or nine years old, Dad took me by the hand, knelt on one knee and showed me pictures of two ladies and asked me which I liked best. I don't know which one I picked, or if that's the one he married, but I know that he married the one that lived next door to his Mom's house and that's how they met, talking over the fence. While visiting with them in Beaumont one summer, we got dressed to go somewhere, Dad took one look at me and said "go powder your face, it's all shiny". I remember looking in the mirror, smiling and thinking he really cares! My sister told me, when I recently told her about it, that he was proud of all of his girls and wanted us to look our best. The last job that he worked at was a bakery. When I got married, he helped to make a beautiful wedding cake for me and held it on his lap all the way to Louisiana. Then he walked me down the aisle. He was also there for my first Communion. He wasn't always there, but he was there when I needed him.

In 1970 I had a dream, I saw my Father standing on top of a high hill, his head was bent down low and there was the huge red sun going down ever so slowly behind him. It was like watching a movie. When I awoke I had a heavy, terrible feeling that I couldn't shake off. When I got busy, it would leave for a while but then return to torment me. After a few days it went away. About a week later my sister called from Louisiana asking could I come to Texas. Dad had a heart attack.

I flew to Texas and the hospital and stayed with him for a week. The Doctor had said that he was doing better and he could go home the following Wednesday. In the meantime, my husband and the kids had driven to come and get me to go back home to Chicago. We left that Wednesday and when we got home, my husband's cousin who had stayed at the house met us at the door and said "I am so sorry to tell you this, but your Father passed away yesterday. They tried to contact you on the freeway through the Highway Patrol but they were unable to make contact with you." So I had to fly right back for the funeral.

When Mom died, I was too young to realize what had happened, but his death was very hard to endure, even though he wasn't always around. I knew that he loved his children, especially his baby girl. About a week later, it hit me like a sudden stroke, that's what the dream was all about, a warning that something bad was about to happen. I have had many such incidences happen in my life.

One summer when it was time to leave Texas and return home to Louisiana, I became depressed and didn't want to go back. I cried most of the way. Some of the women on the train felt sympathetic and kept asking why I cried. I didn't want to tell them the reason. I don't know why (except that I cried so hard,) one woman sitting next to me asked "did you Mom die chere?" I said yes, but she couldn't have known that Mom had died 4 years before. I guess I said yes so she wouldn't ask any more questions. When I arrived at the Train Station in Opelousas, there was no one there to meet me. Of course there were no phones so, I finally asked a cab driver to take me to Grandma Briscoe's house which was nearby. She and T-taunt Lorina and the kids were happy to see me, and I was happy to see familiar faces. I stayed with them a few days. We went shopping and Auntie had to pay some bills. Then she bought ice cream for the kids. After a few days I wanted to go home, I missed my family. It finally occurred to me that I could write a letter for them to come and get me. That was one of the few times I got a complement, they said that was a smart thing to do.

MOMON BROUSSARD

My Grandmother Emelena Broussard's husband had died many years before. After he died, my Grandmother and I lived with my oldest sister Madelle and her family. I was not aware of anything Creole until I entered grade school and Grandma kept calling other people "English" people. At that time I didn't want to speak Creole because as it were, I was teased because I had light skin and to speak the language would be admitting that I was different.

She was proud of the fact that she was born free. She'd say *"ja ane lebre ea majore"* although we weren't sure what she meant by *majore*, we knew that *lebre* meant (free or librated), so we just accepted that she was telling the truth. She was my main source of information and she kept a close rein on me so I wouldn't get in *traka,* trouble.

My boyfriend and I didn't go out on dates. Instead, we stayed home, talked, and sometimes played card games. My dear Grandmother would sit behind a closed door within hearing range and listened to what was going on between us. One night she walked in on us, my boyfriend had his arm behind me on the couch, not touching me, but he was surprised and removed his arm, she accused him of touching me and called him all kinds of names in Creole which embarrassed him, because he understood what she said. He stood up to leave, but my brother-in-law told him not to be offended, so he stayed.

Grandmon had a large armoire in her bedroom and inside the door there was one drawer in which she kept her finest linens and collectibles and in the second one she kept cookies and orange candy slices for obedient children that did chores for her. She would pay me to iron her clothes but she wanted me to iron them a certain way. I was stubborn and wanted to do it my way. I wish I could go back and do such little things for her, when she loved me and did so much for me.

Madelle had nine children, so grandma took care of all the children *"tou leas efant."* One day as she watched the younger kids playing in the hot sun, and called out "get un the sun get un the shate" meaning get out of the sun get in the shade.

That was the extent of her English and my Creole was not much better at that time. She got very upset with me one day and said *"pour qoui te pal pa Creole, te pal pa bien Engalis comain."* "Why don't you speak Creole? You don't speak good English anyway."

When I got married, my husband and I lived for a while with his mother Idelle, who spoke no English, so I learned to speak Creole fluently with her. The first time I visited my husband's family I realized that I was getting into another Creole family, when I heard his youngest sister speak Creole at seven years old. Once I heard her speaking Creole while crying and arguing with her brother. I love it when I go home and meet someone that can hold a conversation in Creole. Sometimes I think that I am one of the few people left that still can. I know some real French and some Spanish, but for me, the Creole language describes the way Creole people live.

My stepmother Hilma asked me to call her "mother". I didn't mind because I didn't have a Mother so I taught it would be okay. But I did not in front of my sisters because they didn't care for her very much, except for Madelle, who admonished them saying we should respect her because she was good for Dad. Hilma was nice to me. On Sundays we would have chocolate cake and Ne-Hi orange soda, because she knew how much I liked it. On my 13th birthday she bought a pretty dress for me and we had our pictures taken. She sent me a birthday card every year until she died. The only problem I had with her was that she always said she had a headache when some one came to visit. We taught that she was faking, but later when she had a stroke; we realized that the headaches were the symptoms of a stroke. She lived many years without the use of her right side.

TEENAGE YEARS

When I attended Holy Ghost Catholic School, I was living with my sister Genevie and her husband just out side of Opelousas city limits in a house that my dad owned. At that time we lived near Grandma Briscoe and her daughter, T-taunt Lorina, who had children about my age, and some other cousins so we "hung out together". There was an open field in back of the house, where we would escape to when no one was looking.

In that area we once saw a family of American Indians under a Tent (not a Teepee). There was a canal that ran on the side of our house, so I guess they lived there to be near the water. Of course we were interested, because they looked and lived differently from the way we did. The Mother was cooking over an open fire. We stared at them for a while but were told to leave. Soon after they moved away, but we saw where they moved to, on a wide open piece of land known as the Airport (we never did see any airplanes there though). We went to see if we could find them, and when we did, we were told to leave and never come back.

While living in that same house and returning from Holy Ghost School one day, there was an old man that chased me and some school friends about a half block, we ran into an old grocery store that had a powerful smell of shrimp (I think they sold dried shrimp). The owners were two big fat women, they were nice to us and threatened the old man with a broom and said they would call the cops if they saw him around children again.

Afterwards I continued to walk toward home in fear, but I was relieved when I saw my Aunt's house that was on the same street, I decided that I needed and deserved a break after what I had been through. She saw me and invited me to come in for a visit. My

Aunt had a daughter-in law that lived with her while her husband was in the service. While we were talking, the daughter-in law started having a seizure and was thrashing and rolling all over the floor. I was terrified but Aunt Therese knew what to do, since this was not the first time that had happened. She wanted me to help hold her down. I was willing to help but it was impossible for me to hold her. Fortunately, Uncle John walked in just in time to take her to the hospital.

In the meantime my sister and her husband were looking for me and happened to stop by my Aunt to see if she had seen me go by and were relieved to see that I was OK. I recounted to them what had happened about the old man at the store. They went to the store to get more information about the incident and took me to school for a while. Not long afterwards I went to live with my sister Madelle in the country.

When we went to school in the country, some of my nieces and I walked to school together, and along the way school buses would pass us by with the white kids, who called us names and would throw stuff at us. My brother-in-law and some other men got together and bought some kind of old half truck and half bus that we rode in for a while, until it stopped running. According to Brother Joel the driver had to put his foot through the floor board to make it stop (à la Flintstones).

After leaving Holy Ghost School in the city, I attended public school but I got married before I graduated. I was always determined to complete high school. After getting divorced, I was able to attend

Platt College, a small business and technical school in Denver.

LEAVING LOUISIANA

My husband and I had two children, Mary Catherine and Stanley Paul. We left Louisiana reluctantly when my husband Paul, went to work for a construction company that moved to different states. We moved about six times while the kids were in school. It was a learning experience for them. We made a lot of friends and lost some along the way. The smallest city we lived in was Coolville, Ohio where the post office was also a grocery store and a gas station.

While traveling, my husband and I spoke Creole so the kids would not understand what we were saying while we tried to decide where to stop for food or rest. My five year old daughter made the remark that, there were only two words she needed to know in Creole and that was "*monge* and *l'argon*," which mean "eat and money." Stan's only concern was, "did he have to kiss all those old ladies when we got home to Louisiana."

The old ladies, especially Grandma, were so happy to see us when we arrived to see the family. They would give us a big kiss and a bear hug, then push us back and say "let me look at you, Ahhh main ta mag, ta malade?" (You so skinny, are you sick?). Or it could be "you look good, you're fat and healthy." Grandma didn't know anything about eating healthy, she was seventy four. Fat was good in those days, if not good for you.

She was so healthy, she could press a pair of jeans by folding and sitting on them for a while and they came out "bien bon" according to her, as she laughed.

Grandma passed away in her sleep in 1955.

CREOLE FOODS AND RECIPES

Once I was sent home while the others were working in the fields, to cook dinner (we ate the heavy meals at noon), I made a roux gravy, added some sliced Irish potatoes and dropped some eggs in it, unfortunately the gravy was thick enough to cut with a knife and the eggs were too hard to eat. We settled for scrambled eggs and rice.

Rice is grown in Louisiana, so it is a staple used in, or served with many dishes. We also made a type of sausage called *boudin* that comes from the French word to stuff. Sausage casings were used to stuff a mixture of pork, liver, onions, garlic and spices, (from mild to very hot), then mixed with rice.

In the month of October or November, there was a *butcheere*. That's when pigs were slaughtered. I would hide in the house and cover my ears with a pillow so I wouldn't have to hear the pigs squealing. Families that lived nearby and neighbors would come together to help kill, clean, cook and have some to take home. Some parts of the meat were used for different purposes, including hams, sausages, *boudin* or a roast. There was always a man from the agriculture extension service that was there to make sure the process was done safely.

He was big and fat and the kids always felt that he ate too much at the *bucheere.*

In everyday life we learned to cook some of the best foods in the country, along with what we learned from the Africans and the American Indians, who used the sassafras roots to reduce fever, and some of it was ground very fine and used to flavor Gumbo, (which is a an African name). Of course, I am biased when it comes to Creole food. In the winter, Grand-ma was always ready to heat up a pot of gumbo which she kept in the freezer. This is just some of the more famous and recognized recipes in Louisiana.

CHICKEN AND ANDOUILLE SAUSAGE GUMBO

Gumbo is not is not a soup, as some would like to believe. It begins with a roux which is made with flour and oil, stirred until dark brown, preferably in a cast iron pot or heavy skillet. The word roux is a French word for rust colored and it gives the Gumbo a nutty, smoky flavor, but is primarily a thickener.

Use 2 cups of oil and 2 cups of flour. You can double or triple this recipe; it keeps for months in the fridge.

You have to stir this constantly on medium heat until it's a dark brown.

There is a joke in Louisiana that say's "If the house starts to burn, do not stop stirring the roux." You should have it on medium heat, and do not leave it for a second, it burns easily. Transfer it to a large pot. Let it cool for a while. Add 1 quart of hot water to the roux and continue stirring it over low heat, it can burn at the bottom of the pot even with the liquid. Add the balance of liquid or stock according to how many servings you need. Stir to be sure the roux and liquid mixes thoroughly.

CHICKEN AND SAUSAGE JUMBALIA

I use precooked chicken from grocery store or fast food place, it is well seasoned, I remove the skin and fat. It saves a lot of time by not having to cut and brown it first.

3 lbs of chicken
1 lb smoked sausage
¼ cup chopped onions
¼ cup chopped green onions
¼ cup chopped celery
¼ chopped bell pepper
2 cloves chopped garlic
1-8 ounce can stewed tomato
1 ½ cups chicken broth
½ teaspoon sugar
¼ dried thyme
1 bay leaf
2 bags of success rice, boiled in the bag and completely cooled

Cut sausages in to bite size pieces and brown them. In the same pan, sauté the onions, celery, bell peppers, add parsley and add the garlic last. Then add the chicken, sausage, and remaining ingredients. Stir. Bring just to a boil, reduce heat to a simmer and cook uncovered until it's thoroughly done (about 25 minutes). Cover and add more liquid broth if liquid evaporates too quickly. Season to taste with Tony Chachere's seasoning, it should be spicy. If it looks too greasy, tilt the pot and skim the top off with a spoon. Then add the cooled rice to the hot mixture, if too hot, the rice will get mushy. Stir thoroughly. Serve with mixed green salad.

BENYEAS

A wonderful little crispy ball of deep fried dough that Creoles loves to have with their coffee or just as treat with syrup, jam or just cover with powdered sugar.

Mix 1 stick of butter, 1/8 teaspoon salt, and 1 cup of water in a sauce pan and boil the mixture until the butter melts. Remove from the heat and add 1 cup flour. Beat with a wooden spoon until the mixture forms a ball that pulls away from the side of the pan. When it has cooled, add 4 eggs, one at a time, beating the mixture smooth after each egg. Stir in 1 tablespoon of sugar. Add 1 teaspoon each of lemon and orange peel or flavoring. Drop the dough by tablespoons full in hot oil, preferably in a fry pot about 10 to 12 minutes or until golden brown. Drain on paper towels.

CUSH-CUSH

We grew corn on the farm, so we made a hot cereal, called Cush-Cush by mixing 2 cups corn meal, add a teaspoon baking powder, a pinch of salt. Add just enough water to mix well. Grease the bottom of a cast iron pot and spread the mixture all over the bottom of the pot, let it brown on that side then, turn it over and brown on the other side. Break it up with a large spoon, stir until it gets crumbly. Cover and let steam about ten minutes on low heat, serve with milk.

My oldest sister, Madelle

My second sister, Edith

My third sister, Geneva

My fourth sister, Eunice

My third brother, Sidney

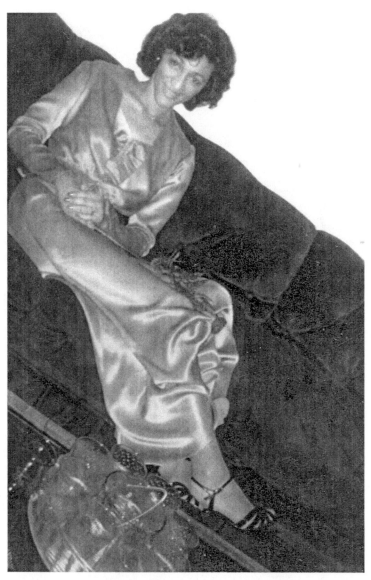

My sixth (youngest) sister, Hilda Anne

RULES AND REGULATIONS

I didn't mind house work, but if I found something interesting to read, I would stop for a while and take a break, until Madelle came in and said I was like our neighbor who never got her housework done. I was always very impressed when she'd say "what kind of parent would I be if I didn't teach you this and let you get away with that…" (what ever I did wrong). That made a lot of sense, but why did it always have to be when I was having fun? One of the things she hated most was if we walked over some item on the floor. It went something like this, "I can't believe you walked over that piece of clothing on the floor and didn't pick it up."

To this day I can't resist picking up stuff on the floor, even in the grocery store where other people might ignore it. I see some thing on the floor ahead of me and I think to my self, I am not going pick it up, but I do. Another one of her favorites was "If you see something that needs to be done, do it, don't wait to be told."

We always enjoyed watching Madelle in action when one of her seven girls got on her last nerve. She would call out three or four names before she got the attention of the guilty party, Ann Marie, Juanita, Juba, then she got frustrated, stomped her foot, raised her voice and say "you know who I am talking to" I believe she expected the child to raise her hand and say "OK it was me Mother, I did it." The other girls were Bernadine,

Beatrice, Margaret and Christine. Her husband felt that their two boys, Lionel and Joey, could do no wrong.

Madelle would actually blush if someone even mentioned anything about having babies. We were ordered out of the room while the conversation was going on. Madelle passed away in 1994, she was the only person I knew as my mother and I took it very hard when she passed, I live by the lessons she thought me and I've always strived to emulate her.

THINGS TO DO IN OPELOUSAS

Of course there wasn't much to do in a small town like Opelousas, Louisiana. We were not yet old enough to go to a Zydeco dances. We went to Church, visited cousins and friends, maybe a wedding, or met at funerals. The most fun was the annual church bazaars. If the crops were good that year, we might even have a new dress to wear and show off. My girlfriends and I would walk arm in arm or join hands and walk around the building continuously, to make sure we didn't miss anything, like who was smooching; who was talking to whom; could we put our money together to buy something or play a game of bingo and who would get the prize if we won?

Another one of my favorite occasions was the annual October Yambalee which is held in my favorite town of Opelousas, to give recognition to the lowly sweet potato or yam. I marched in the parade as a young teen. There are too many Festivals to name. Some of my favorites are the Zydeco Festival, Crawfish Festival and Acadiana Festival, held in Opelousas and the Creole Festival in Natchitoches Area in Cane River Country.

We attended a small church where we were able to see everything that was going on inside. We didn't pay enough attention to the mass because we were too busy giggling. This particular Sunday, feeling no guilt or shame we laughed at a woman's hat, but when we got home we found that my sister's hat was on backwards. We had a good laugh. I guess that was karma at work, or as Madelle would say "do unto others"… (the golden rule).

Like a lot of people, we had one pair of shoes that we wore every day and another pair for Sunday and special occasions well, I decided to ignore the rule and wore the good shoes every day even to school, when that pair wore out I wanted another one, but instead I had to wear the same shoes all the time, until I learn my lesson and did what was expected. Madelle said that only negligent, lazy people walked on the heel of their shoes, because they were too lazy to take the time to put them on properly. When ever I see the shoes that are popular now, with no heel cover, I smile because no one has to walk on the heel cover of their shoes any more.

My cousin Marie Brookter challenged the Quaker Oats Company to remove the *teyon* from Aunt Jemima who was portrayed as black (the original Aunt Jemima was white) but they wanted to sell more of their products to blacks. Marie had at one time worked at the White

House. I must confess I didn't really believe her until I saw papers that proved it.

A similar story is that, as early as 1786 a law was passed in an effort to have the quadroons (who looked white) recognized as women of color, were made to wear *teyons* wrapped around their heads, but the women used it to their advantage by using beautiful colorful cloths, adorning them with flowers and jewels.

When we repeat something Madelle said, or did, we call it Madelle-ism. I remember one Sunday we were riding along in a car on a country road, where we saw two siblings fighting as if their lives depended on it, in their front yard. We stopped and waited to see if someone would come out of the house, then pulled them apart and stopped the fight. The next time my sister saw the parents, she told them what had happened. I was afraid that they might get angry, but instead they said how much they appreciated it and said thank you. I was hoping they wouldn't tell them but I know now it was the right thing to do.

My second oldest brother, Joel

BROTHER JOEL

My brother Joel should have been a comedian, or maybe he is. He can make a serious joke about anyone and make them laugh. He tells the story about his niece who lived alone. One night she awoke to find a man crawling around on her floor on his hands and knees. When he realized that she was awake he ran out the door, she chased after him saying "stop, come back, I won't call the cops, I just want to talk." The first part is true.

Joel and I are a few years apart, but I remember a lot of his antics. He was not only funny but also smart. As children, sometimes on Saturday's we were allowed to go fishing for crawfish, he would take a small piece of any kind of meat available, tie a string on a stick and catch as many as we could. But first Joel would make a chimney on the inside wall of a ditch by making a large hole on the top of the ditch, then dig through the side under the top opening and build a fire with twigs. He would use an old pot or any kind of can, boil the water, then put the crawfish in. Some times we would pick black berries in the same area, add a bit of sugar that he swiped from the kitchen and we'd enjoy a wonderful desert after the crawfish. When the day was over and the Cicadas and Crickets seem to be in harmony, in the cool night air, we would lie on our backs on the porch and, he'd show me the constellation and the stars but especially the big dipper. He'd say "don't you see the handle and the cup of the dipper?"

Once when my sister and her husband left us alone while going to the city for supplies and take care of business, Joel got so excited thinking of all the mischief he could get into, he did a jig, kicked his foot in the air and a heavy, untied shoe flew right into a window pane and needless to say, smashed the glass to smithereens, he picked up the broken glass in the palm of his hand, held it to the window and said "Oh God, paleeeeese put this glass back together before they get home." That's one time that he was very serious.

We had a tractor to use on the farm and Joel thought it was a good idea to let me learn to drive it into the barn where it was stored for the night. I got on it and drove it right through the back wall! Fortunately it was a very old building, so I didn't get hurt. I wasn't always innocent. When I was about five I actually broke a bottle on Joel's head, while we were playing on the floor. I don't recall why I thought he deserved that, but it must have been a soft bottle because he laughed after the initial shock.

As children we didn't have the usual toys or pets like dogs and cats, we had one horse and two mules. The horse was used for riding and going to the store. The mules were used for farming and doing the hard tasks. Like humans they had different personalities. Stella was reddish color, the larger of the two. Ella was smaller and brown with a quite disposition. Once when I was left at home with the younger kids, Stella decided to escape and went for an excursion in the wide open spaces of the pasture. I chased her all over the pasture and finally got her back into the pen. She turned and looked at me with a look that, seem to say "now that was fun." Ella seemed happy that she was back.

We lived at the end of a dusty road, about a half mile from the nearest grocery store where I was sent once in a while to purchase something of immediate need. Not wanting to go alone, I asked for my niece, Ann Marie, to accompany me and along the way a piece of wire got stuck in her bare foot. After removing the wire I brought her all the way home on my back. But we did get laganppe, (a little something extra from the store), usually a lollipop or some type of candy. Of course we also had cows which I tried to milk once, but wound up on the ground with milk all over me when she kicked her leg and decided that was enough.

There was and old man that use to drive around the neighborhood in a dilapidated old truck that was opened in back and was stocked with simple items such as thread, needles and other household items. The kids would watch for him on certain days and called out on his approach so Madelle could be ready to purchase what she needed.

RELIGION

In 1842 the congregation of the Sisters of the Holy Family founded their own order for nuns. Convents were closed to blacks. Henrette DeLille Sarpy was the daughter of Jean DeLille Sarpy, who was French and Italian. Her mother was African American, Spanish and French, which makes Henrette Creole. She was able to fulfill her dream of becoming a nun, and with the help of a white woman and other free women of color, she opened a church, school and an orphanage. Since that time there has been a proposal for her canonization for Sainthood (Mary Gehman, *The Free People of Color of New Orleans*).

Mother Cabrini was not Creole but an Italian immigrant who founded the Sisters of the Sacred Heart and became the first American citizen to be named a saint by the Catholic Church. In1892 she visited New Orleans. A building in New Orleans known as the Pitot House was owned by Mother Cabrini and the sisters of the Sacred Heart and used as their convent for many years. She heard about the poverty of the Italian immigrants in the slums around Saint Phillip Street. They were considered low class hoodlums; eleven of them were lynched and murdered shortly before she arrived. They pleaded for her to open a Church for them. She also set up an Orphanage and a High School for girls. In 1902, Mother Cabrini arrived in Denver, Colorado by invitation of Bishop Nacholas Matz. She was criticized for visiting the Italians who worked in the mines and for riding on horseback. In her honor, there is a Shrine that she helped build on the side of the Rocky Mountain with 373 steps to reach the top, where there is a 22 foot stature of the Sacred Heart, encircled by a wall adorned with the Ten Commandments, the Stations of the Cross and mysteries of the Rosary. It is said that while she was there and needing water she struck a rock and water flowed. At that sight there is a fountain where water is still available. There are also several chapels where it is possible to light candles and pray.

There is a church in Isle Berville, Louisiana known as St. Augustines. The first recorded history of St. Augustine Church states that on July 19, 1829 St. Augustine Chapel was blessed by Reverend J. B. Blanc, Pastor of St. Francis Church in Isle Brevelle, Louisiana. The chapel was proclaimed to be a mission church to the Parish of St. Francis. It was named in honor of Augustin's patron saint, St. Augustine, who was a great scholar and Bishop of Hippo. On March 11, 1856 the mission of St Augustine was established as a parish church. Bishop Auguste Martin of the Diocese of Natchitoches issued the decree and named his brother, Father Francois Martin as the first resident priest of the new Parish Church. In 1913 the Holy Ghost Order was asked to serve in the Diocese. They served the Parish until 1990. From that time to present day the Parish is served by the diocesan priest of Alexandria, Louisiana. The present structure was erected in 1916 and recently underwent a major expansion and renovation.

St. Augustine was the first Catholic Church in America founded, independently financed, and built by free people of color. The Church still serves as the spiritual and social center of the community and remains a shelter of stability for their deep faith and unique culture. A portrait of Augustin Metoyer believed to be the oldest existing painting of an American of color, done by an American of color, painter J. Feuille of New Orleans.

The Tomb of Augustin Metoyer and his wife Marie Agnes are located in the cemetery directly behind the church. The wrought iron grave markers in the cemetery are nineteenth century French inscribed crosses. The painting of St. Augustine is the same that hung in the original church. The bell in the Church tower is the original that was used in the first Church.

The annual fall Church fair is a fund raising event and celebration that draws people from across the country for authentic Creole cuisine and dancing to Zydeco music. They also offer a website to search for your ancestors and have a chance to show your skill at speaking Creole. This event is held every year on the second weekend of October. The All Saints Day candle light celebration is an annual event which brings survivors of those buried in the cemetery together for prayer and reflection. The priest leads a candlelight procession from the church through the cemetery that concludes with the candles being placed at the family tombs. (Janet Revere Colson).

DENVER, COLORADO

In 1975 my husband, Paul, the kids and I came to visit my three brothers in Denver, not having been raised together except for Joel, before he joined the military at Fort Carson I desperately wanted to live near my family since we couldn't live in Louisiana. When leaving Denver we stopped along the highway to have a last glance of snow capped Rocky Mountains. It was then that I made up my mind that Denver was the place I wanted to live. And since my marriage was already in trouble, I was thinking of making a life there for myself and my children.

After getting divorced and moving to Denver, I needed to work. I got a position with Samsonite Corporation in quality control. After working nine years, I sustained an injury that damaged my muscles to the point where I could hardly sit and had to quit the job. I was accused of faking the injury and was sent to a psychiatrist, where I learned a lot about myself and at the end of the session, he said that I should be insane after all that I had gone through since I was a child and that someone must be looking out for me.

I decided to go into child care and while checking the want ads I happen to see a position near my home. While still considering other options, I drove by the address that was in the paper and noticed that it was the same as my birth date.

Being "sensitive" and intuitive I decided this must be the place where I should be. There were three boys, Nathen 12, Vincent 5 and Nicky, who was only two. Because Nicky was just a baby, I guess I paid more attention to him than Vincent. In fact I rocked Nicky to sleep every day in an antique rocker until it broke. Vincent cried each day when his Mom left for work and got so angry with me, he rammed into me head first and I fell. Along with the muscle damage I already had, I wasn't fit for much of anything afterwards.

The children's father, George, and his wife Christene, insisted that I see a doctor that they knew. After examinations, the diagnosis was lymphoma cancer. So you see if Vincent hadn't knocked me down (I was already in the fourth stage) I may not be writing this now and I am inclined to agree, as he says, that he saved my life. I continued to take care of the kids while having chemo treatments and for a while, they took care of me. But while having what's known as a buffalo stuck in my arm (because my veins were so hard to find) to attach the needle without sticking me again, when at home I was able to refinish a whole bedroom set, because the doctor didn't want me to have too much spare time on my hands to think about my condition. That was eleven years ago.

The oncologist that treated me was amazed at how fast I improved with treatment. He walked up to me and said, "Some one must be watching over you," as he pointed his thumb upwards. Later one of the young nurses came over and said that the doctor who made that remark was not a believer. While waiting for test results, brother Joel and I went for lunch, he seemed scared and downhearted. I thought I could make him laugh when I jokingly said, "well, there's always Doctor Kevorkian." He gave me a look that made me wish I hadn't said it and he got up and walked away.

We all have to die with something but I would hate to leave my children and grandchildren. When I found out that I had to sit for long periods of time while the chemotherapy did its thing, I went to a book store to get something to read, it was then that I saw a book about Creoles by Mary Gehman called *The Free People of Color of New Orleans*. I called her and she's the person that has encouraged and helped me to start this book. There are many bad things that happened in my life, but I've read somewhere that "all things happen for good, for those who love the Lord," and I can certainly claim that. Cancer has taught me to appreciate people wherever they are; do all that I can to help others and accept who they are; take better care of my self, eat healthy and exercise; have a positive attitude about life; and remember the prayer of St. Francis of Assisi:

God grant me the serenity to accept the things I cannot change, the courage to change the things I can, and the wisdom to know the difference.

I believe that God sends people into our lives, at just the right time to help us, but if it doesn't happen the way we want it to, then it is not what he had planned for us.

LE CREOLE

The word Creole causes so much misunderstanding and confusion because many people do not understand where the word came from. In the beginning the French and Spanish people called their children Creoles because they were born in the new land of America, in New Orleans. Later some one decided that mixed people of color, born in the new land were not African, French, or Spanish but, a mixture of all three, they were a new creation of people defined by a new culture of their own. They were created in the new land, so they were a new race created by God and man.

The French culture gave us the Catholic religion, the French dialect and *joiore devie*, love of life. The Spanish gave us the beautiful architecture in New Orleans. Native Americans taught us how to use sassafras to reduce fever, some of it is ground very fine to flavor and season gumbo.

This book is about Creoles, but I must honor my black heritage. Our black culture makes us strong and able to withstand hardships. Even to this day Creoles are accused of not wanting to be called black if they speak of their history and culture. In writing about Creoles, it is not my intention to deny my black heritage. I have a friend who said I should be proud of who I am. My response was, I am proud of who I am. But she meant that I should be proud of being black. I explained that I have part of the black race in me and I am proud of it and that's what makes me a Creole.

We cannot nor do we want to ignore our black brothers and sisters. We all suffered and some died, trying to win our civil rights which we all have today. Some Creoles "passed" for white, in order to have the advantage of better jobs and social standing and to avoid the prejudices that were exacted upon blacks.

In 1812, a law was passed preventing any articles to be printed in favor of blacks and slaves and that they should not be educated. During slavery and many years later many whites and blacks helped slaves escape the harsh reality of slavery through what is known as the underground railroad to Canada and other areas. In spite of all the harassment, jails and bloodshed, this day in the twenty first century we have a black President of the United States, Barack Obama.

Until Junior High School I was called Frenchie and Geegiee and every thing except Creole, at that time I didn't know much about my culture to explain who I really am. After a friend of mine read my manuscript she said that she understood the Creole culture much better. It's kind of strange that there are some blacks and whites that want Creoles to say that they are not Creole, but in reality 95% of all blacks in America have white blood in their veins, they are not pure African even though they were taken from Africa. *Africa began the race of civilization and human progress*...Harriet Becher Stowe.

In 1791 the Haitian revolution brought more than 10,000 Creoles of French, African and mixed descent to Louisiana and Spain cedes Louisiana to France. The French and the Spanish people mixed blood, so that is why they called their children Creoles.

Then they mixed with blacks and (we have the French names to prove it). The Spanish culture is not as prevalent, but there are Creoles who have Spanish names and some Creoles actually live in Mexico. It is the mixed cultures, not the color that makes a Creole. It's like a pot of Gumbo with mixed ingredients.

Martin Luther King said *"People should not be judged by the color of their Skin, but by the content of their character"*.

We are not trying to take away a possession from some one, it is what it is, a word, a French culture mixed with Black and Spanish. It is a historical fact, any one in doubt should look it up, do the research, we did. I think it's crucial that we document and preserve our heritage and language so that our children will know where they came from. "People without a past are people without a future." (Gerald N.Grob and George Athan Billias, *Interpretation of American History*).

The Creole culture is unique, in the way we worship, the language we speak, the food we eat and the music that we love to dance to, known as Zydeco. In spite of the uniqueness of this culture, some non Creoles refuse to admit that we even exist, including one New York person who said he had never heard of a Creole.

You may not recognize a Creole person by the color of their skin, which ranges from pale to very dark, but listen to the way they speak for a while and you'll hear that Creole accent and hear them speak some Creole words without trying to. Ask a Creole if something is good and sometimes they'll say "may yea" or "yea sha" Some of the older people use English and Creole together like "say sa I want to know" (that's what I want to know).

BOUDREAUX'S BOOK OF JOKES

Budreaux was married to Marie, they lived across the Bayou from Clarence. They had been enemies for many years. After the State of Louisiana built a bridge across the Bayou, Marie said to her husband Boudreaux, now is the time to go over there and beat up Clarence. Boudreaux said OK. So he goes half way on that bridge and went back home. Marie asked, did you beat him up good? Non he said, I go half way on that bridge and I see a big sign that say Clearance, 13ft. When I see him cross that Bayou he don't look that big non.

In Creole:

Boudreaux ea marriea aveck Marie, ea resta lortha boord da-l Bayou da Cleronce. Le deau hiesa Cloronce. Aprea de ton La-Ataa da la Louisanne ah beta an pon ke va lort boord da-l Bayou. Marie dea ah sonn marrie "sa ton tee va la ba ea bechea Cloronce" Brodeaux dee OK. E va a la mochea da-la pon. Toot suite ea retoun , Marie mond "tee la bechea bien?"

Boudreaux dee non, ja etae la mochee dal-pon, ea ja vee an gron signe ke dee "treize piea". Con ja-la vee lorte boord dal-pon, ea gordea pa gron com sa non.

THE CULTURE

When a Creole baby is born Catholic, as soon as possible he or she is taken to church to be baptized. The Godparents are called Nanan and Paran. They are suppose to help look after the child, along with the parents and see that they do their Christian duty, like making their first communion, confirmation and grow up to be good, strong Christians and sometimes giving them gifts or money.

For weddings, there is a full course meal and all cakes made from scratch, except for the wedding cake. With help from all the female relatives, as many as ten cakes were made depending on how many guests they expected. Sometimes there were competitions as to who made the best and prettiest cake. Some of the fillings used for the cakes were coconut, pineapple, chocolate and even jelly. The men would take a gallon of wine, add water and a little sugar and what you wound up with was some kind of punch that even the kids could have.

You've heard of Southern hospitality, but Creoles take it further. At most homes you will be fed whether you're hungry or not. You got to eat. While you're eating you hear "hep you sef" you don't eat much non, take some home to eat later. They are generally genteel and afraid to hurt any one's feelings. I knew a man that started his sentence with "no harm cus but," meaning "I don't want to hurt your feelings but I am going to tell you how it is."

The Creole children "<u>used</u>" to respect their elders. I think they still say "yes Mam and yes Sir." When I was young I never hear a Creole say "I am poor, loan me some money," they were too proud. Most Creole women cooked three times a day, if they didn't work outside the home. I love to cook and entertain. As children we were forbidden to eat at anyone's house, they might think we didn't have any food at home. The women always served their husband a plate of food first, the children next and she sat down to eat last. Coffee was served in demi-tas which is a (half size cup) usually very strong, sometimes with Chicory and lots of sugar. If you gave them a mug of coffee, they would look at it and say "what is this, I can see the bottom of the cup, is it tea?"

Creoles should not be confused with Cajuns, who are white, but like Creoles they share a French Catholic Heritage. They were expelled from Nova Scotia by the British government in 1770. Many of them wound up in Southwest Louisiana and have their own type of spicy foods. They speak a French dialect similar to Creole and enjoy dancing to lively fiddle and accordion music. They took the family to what they called a (fai doa-doa) meaning put to sleep, because they would put the children in a room to sleep while they danced. The soft music was supposed to lull them to sleep.

Like other groups living in Louisiana some Cajuns have mixed through generations with Native Americans, black and white Creoles. With this mixture has become a blur of culture and racial lines. Because of segregation laws in the past and continued prejudices that still exist, Creoles have not had the attention that Cajuns have.

The Creoles were in Louisiana in 1719, long before the Cajuns arrived in 1785. In spite of information written and published by Creoles, they have been overlooked by mainstream history books. After the Civil War, when all people were technically free, the term "Creoles of color" appeared to cover non-whites, who shared a common history and culture with those of French and Spanish background.

In the 1880s a New Orleans native, George Washington Cable, who was white, wrote several short stories about the black Creoles of Louisiana from the1800s in which he made fun of the stuffy customs of the whites and praised the free blacks. It was very popular in the North, but his writings were banned by white Creoles and he had to leave Louisiana.

Many Creoles left Louisiana and moved to California, Houston and other cities for jobs and better living conditions. They have kept the Creole culture. Unfortunately the younger generation has lost the language, but they cannot lose the accent. Whenever I start to speak to a non Creole person, almost immediately they ask "where are you from?"

When you consider the skills and talents of millions of Creoles and their descendants who have left New Orleans and Louisiana, through the centuries seeking acceptance and equality in other parts of the country, it is mind boggling how Creoles have stayed together and seem to find each other through churches and Zydeco clubs where the music that is so familiar to most of them. But also through jobs and in part, by the successes they have achieved in almost every possible situation and profession.

Even though there appears to be few ongoing connections between Creoles in New Orleans and countries where they moved to in large numbers in the eighteenth and nineteenth centuries, such as Haiti, Cuba, Mexico and France, Creole communities exist in every part of the United States.

The largest population of Creoles outside New Orleans is in Los Angeles where many families migrated, first in the late 1930's and early 1940's because of wartime industries that were hiring workers there and in the late1940's and early 1950s as blacks sought refuge from segregation in Louisiana. The Sunset Limited, a train that still runs the two thousand miles between New Orleans and Los Angeles, became a line of communication for many years. Creoles working on the train would describe the "promised land" of southern California to friends and family. In the 1950s, there was even a stretch of Jefferson, Boulevard in Los Angeles called Little New Orleans.

THE MUSIC AND DANCE

The music that Creoles dance to is known as Zydeco. It is a very lively dance, played by an accordion, rub board, guitar and drums. There has always been a discussion as to who first introduced the accordion to Louisiana.

When Zydeco became famous it was like a house afire, an unbelievable craze that took over church basements and old buildings that became Zydeco clubs all over Southwest Louisiana and other states. If you haven't been on a trail ride, where Zydeholics ride on horses and trucks and wagons filled with hay while the bands plays, you have missed a good time.

They play Zydeco music while going down a path for a certain distance and if that's not enough, they take you to a club to enjoy all kinds of great Creole foods. But you don't necessarily have to dance in the club we danced in the house, or outside on the grass.

It started in the 1930s in an era when black Creoles were destitute, trying to make a living as best they could, when the accordion was introduced and they started playing a bluesy type of melody and also waltzes. The music goes back to early 18th century, and was passed onto the French Louisiana settlers and their slaves. But even before that time the slaves were allowed to have Saturday nights to dance in their cabins. That music was not Zydeco, it was danced to with a slow two step. These days, the Zydeco dancers develop their own steps as they go along, depending on how the music makes them feel.

In Denver, Colorado where I live, the Zydeholics think nothing of taking a plane to Louisiana, California or anywhere there is Zydeco music. I must confess I am one of them. There are also Zydeco groups online to savor the activities that are happening at any given time. We bring in bands from other cities in Louisiana to Denver. If it weren't for the Cajun and Zydeco Club in Denver I might have to move back to Louisiana.

Cajun dances were off limits to blacks during segregation, but they would hire the bands to play, which caused a lot of problems, as when a black musician (Amedie Ardion) was beaten and left for dead on the road because a white woman wiped his face with her handkerchief. One Cajun was heard to say that he would like to be black just one Saturday so he could have fun the way they do.

These days it's all a mixture of Creoles, Whites, Latinos and any one that enjoys that type of music with the infectious beat and if you don't dance you will tap your feet ("I garontee!").

When I started going to Zydeco dances, there were certain rules between men and women that were strictly adhered to, except when some one tried something different and caused havoc. For instance, when a guy asked a girl to dance, it was permissible to refuse, but if she danced with someone else on that same (round), he might take offence and approach her in anger and demand the reason for her refusal to him and unless someone intervened there could be an altercation.

Men and women (I should say young people) were never allowed to dance too close together or leave the building. On one particular night, some guy turned off the light switch (it might have been my brother Joel) and the chaperones and mothers started to call out to their daughters "stay where you are." But in the meantime the guy might have stolen a kiss or touched her inappropriately.

But rumor had it that one couple eloped while the lights were out. Once a fight started, the place was cleaned out in no time, because there were instances when knives or guns were involved, but by the time security arrived the weapons were passed around and never found. One of the famous Zydeco clubs was Richard's in Lawtell, Louisiana. Most of the Zydeco bands In Louisiana got their start at Richard's.

There was a different band every Saturday night. These bands now travel all over the United States and many countries overseas. Richard's was the only dance club I attended as a young girl of sixteen, I suppose because the place was owned and operated by my niece, Ann Marie and her husband Kermon Richard. The dances were held every Saturday night, but I went only when my chaperone felt like going. Joel asked Madelle if I could go to the dance with him, she said that could never happen, that he would go on his way and forget about me, so he said he would only leave me for a little while.

One particular night, the decision was made that we should go to another club, where I didn't want to go, because my friends wouldn't be there, it was said that I should go to make new friends. I decided to go but I was determined not to have a good time, so I stood with my arms crossed and the worst expression on my face that I could manage. Well, this guy came up to me and said how "nice" I looked, making fun of me, so I let him ask a few times, then I thought the best way to get rid of him was to dance. When the dance was over he didn't let go of my hand and on the way to the car he pronounced that I was going to be his wife. We saw each other for two years and then got married.

In those days it was customary for intendeds to ask for parent's blessings or actually ask permission to marry. We arrived at his house and the whole family was sitting around waiting for the bomb to drop. My husband's mischievous brother sat there with this big grin on his face knowing how shy I was and every time I tried to start the speech that I had prepared, someone else would start a conversation. At last my fiancée's mother (God bless her), said to me, "Vivian, I know that you came to ask to marry Paul, so you have our blessings," I could have grabbed her and kissed her right at that moment.

When it was his turn, Paul came right to the point: "Mr. and Mrs. Richard, Vivian and I have been seeing each other for two years and I would like your permission to marry her." "Where are you planning to live?" "Well, I have rented a small house on your uncle's property and we will live there until I can get a better job." The wedding was held in the middle of November and even in Louisiana it can be chilly in November. We lived in a medium-size house, but it got so packed with relatives and friends that we wound up having the reception outside, then it started to rain so we had to run back inside.

My husband's parents also had a reception, and on the way, there was an accident when two cars in our group tried to cross a small bridge at the same time. I had a feeling they might have had too much wine punch. So we wound up at the hospital to see the injured. After all that, someone said that the marriage was doomed and it wouldn't last, but it lasted 25 years.

Richard's Zydeco club was in business from 1950 to 2004 when the last heir passed on. It was not the fanciest place on the block or "in the country" but it brought so much joy to so many people. It was said that there were times when, if you weren't on the floor dancing you could feel the vibrations from the gyrating floor moving below you as if you were.

Cars were parked along I-90 in Lawtell for a quarter mile on both sides of the highway and the huge parking lot was full. I remember the excitement I felt when approaching the dance club, just hearing the music I could hardly contain myself. Even though I didn't get to dance every round, it was fun watching others dance. When you walked into the club the first thing you noticed was the heat, especially if it was summer. There were no air conditioners but four large box fans placed in front of each wall, which helped a lot but once you started dancing you forgot the heat and just enjoyed the music and the dancers. You paid a cover charge at the door and proceeded to find the best seat, where you might get a breeze from the fan and if you came without a partner, you checked out the scene to see how many of your relatives and friends were there.

After you meet and greet and ask ("how's you Mom and them?"), you try to find the best place to sit to get a good view of the dance floor and the band, which doesn't last long because, as more people entered the club, your view is blocked by people standing in front of you. If you didn't come with a partner, you wanted to position yourself near the dance floor to make yourself available to be asked to dance. There could be as many as 150 people, so I would sit and talk to anyone within ear shot while the band is warming up before it actually starts.

The excitement builds until you hear the band start the first round. I had eyed a guy that I might like to dance with, but on the way to asking me, some female grabs him and he hates to refuse her, so I sit a few more rounds trying to look like, ("Oh, I didn't really want to dance that round anyway, it was too fast, or too slow."). I start a conversation with someone and just about the time we get a nice chat going, someone ask for a dance. I dance two or three rounds with him, he asked if he might sit with me and would I like a cold drink? By then I feel like I might pass out if I don't, so he takes off and make his way to the bar in front of the club and I wonder if he'll come back.

The music is so intense and loud I feel it inside, as if I might explode if I don't move to the beat. And hey, there's a girlfriend, or maybe she's a cousin and it's Ok for girls to dance together, after all they do that in France. One guy whispers to another, they feel it's not right for two girls to dance together and the next thing I know, I am dancing with the guy who bought the drink. There's something going on in the middle of the crowd that I can't get a good view of. But on closer inspection, it's just one of the best dance couples doing what they do best, dancing to the beat of the best band in Louisiana.

Oh darn there's my ex walking in with a PYT (pretty young thing) on his arm. And there are stares and glares until some peace maker escorts them to the other side of the hall out of sight. I don't know if I am more angry or more hurt, but pleased that I am looking pretty good and glad that there is a guy sitting next to me, (even though I don't know his name). My heart is aching but I can't let him know it. And I am thinking, why did he have to bring her here? Is he trying to make me jealous, I am sure he knew I'd be here. I would like to leave but I don't want him to think that I care.

The guy sitting next to me, ask for a dance and happens to be a friend of the ex, so I made sure to get to the other side of the club where the ex could see us. Finally, I went home, took a shower and had a cup of coffee, because I know I wouldn't sleep any time soon. I wished I had someone to talk to, but I guess I had better get some rest, because I have to get up early for Church in the morning. And back to Zydeco next Saturday night.

GOING TO LOUISIANA

I am revealing this account only because Christmas of 2007, my son wanted to go to Louisiana to see his Father, whom he hadn't seen for quite some time and his sister that had been missing for three and a half years. In the meantime he had gotten married and bought a truck and even though it was a double cab, had not yet purchased a cover for the back to cover luggage. It was snowing in Denver and it always seems to be raining in Houston when we go through there. So it wouldn't be a good idea to travel with the two of them at that time. That was my first unsuccessful time trying to get to Louisiana.

In the process of writing this book and doing research, I wanted to go to Louisiana to visit my family, talk to my sister Edith, who is the eldest living survivor in my family and I thought I could get some information from her about my childhood and growing up. I made reservations through my niece Gala who works for Continental Airlines, to go to Atlanta, Georgia to visit my daughter Catherine. She had fell on hard times when she lost her job and then her home, which affected her very badly, but has since attained a great job and is doing quite well. We would spend time together and then drive to Opelousas where we would visit with the whole family.

I was packed and ready when I heard on the news that a tornado had struck Atlanta. I called and she said that there was no serious damage near her home, but there were trees down and some power outages so we both agreed that maybe it was not a good time for me to go, I would reschedule for another time.

I called Gala and asked if I could go to Houston instead, she said no problem, since I was going through Houston before, to get to Atlanta, that ticket is still open and I could go to Louisiana from there. With my luggage already packed and my ear plugs nearby, I went out for a while and when I returned Gala had left a message that she had forgotten about Spring break and Easter travelers, she didn't think I would be able to get on the plane since I was on standby.

In the meantime the sister that I wanted to see had made her way to Houston. But she had gotten sick and would be leaving that very same day for California. Since she was the one that I really wanted to see in Houston, I wasn't too disappointed. I would call her when she got home. Besides I had one more option. When I explained to my niece Betrice who lives in Denver what had transpired, she said that's OK, because, before I made plans to fly, she had said that I could ride with her and her son since they also were going to drive to Louisiana.

Well, it seems that it was not meant for me to get to Louisiana because just when I was getting excited that I might make it there after all, she called and said that she wouldn't be going, her daughter had been taken to the hospital. That was the third unsuccessful try. Well, that just about did me in. I called my son for some sympathy and ask if he and his wife would take me downtown Denver to be able to change my name from Washington to Malveaux, which was my former name and is the name of my children.

First, I went to the police station to have my fingerprints taken from both hands. I had to send one copy to the FBI and one to the CBI (Colorado Bureau of Investigations). Then we had to go to the City and County Building. I love Denver, but downtown is not the place to go if you're not familiar with it. If you find the address you may have to park several blocks away from it while the meter is running. We fed the meter and walked to the City and County Building. A few steps after we walked in, we had to go through a security gate and put purses and jackets on a conveyer belt and empty our pockets. Then we collected our belongings and headed to the first desk.

I handed the clerk the forms that I had previously filled in. She signed and stamped them and said, "You're late" the judge might have left. She called his office, he was still there, but ready to leave. So she said "go to that window." That guy said, "that will be 108 dollars. Wait here and someone will take you to Courtroom four." We walked down the hallway and the clerk said

Living Creole and Speaking it Fluently

"go through that door and sit down" as she took the papers.

We sat in chairs against the wall and after a few minutes the Judge walked in and sat at his desk, high above where we sat. He took a look at my papers and walked back out. I was starting to get nervous. I didn't know it was such a big deal to change your name. After a few minutes he came out with his black robe on. The clerk said, "Do not stand."

He shuffled some papers and said "Vivian Washington, please come to the podium and speak into the microphone." I said "thanks your Honor for seeing me today, I know that I came in late." "Raise your right hand, do you swear that you are not changing your name to defraud the law, and are there others that might object to your new name?" "No your honor," I replied and almost expected him to say do you swear on this stack of bibles before God and every thing that's holy? "Why do you want to change your name?" I said, "Malveaux is a French name and also the name of my children, I am writing a book about the French Creole culture in Louisiana, so I thought that it would be appropriate to use Malveaux rather than Washington." He smiled and said "I agree and I will grant your petition. Take this to a news paper agency and have them publish your new name 3 times within 21 days." At the *Denver Post* newspaper agency, the cashier said "that will be 45 dollars." That's the process I went through just to have my name changed. I hope I can sell some books to help pay for my expenses.

There are too many famous Creoles to name, but just to name a few: Auxiliary Bishop Dominic Carmon of New Orleans, a relative of my children; Bishop Healy; and Bishop Olivier. There is a petition to the church to make the Creole, Henriette Delille, a saint. Suzanne Malveaux and Bryant Gumble are news reporters on television. Louis Armstrong a famous musician, Fats Domino, and Beyonce are famous R&B singers and there are many, many others.

ZYDECO BANDS

There are too many famous Zydeco bands to name, so I'll name the most recent ones. There's Clifton Chenier, Queen Ida, and Rocking Sidney, all of whom have won Emmys for their music.

Leon Chavis	Buckwheat Zydeco	Geno Delafose
Curley Tayler	Roy Carrier	Leroy Thomas
Keith Frank	T-Broussard	Diki-do

YOU KNOW YOU'RE FROM SOUTH WEST LOUISIANA WHEN:

(*New Orleans Times Picayune*)
- You know you're Creole from Louisiana, when you have God parents called Nanan and Parin.
- You understood Creole as a child, even though you couldn't speak it.

Living Creole and Speaking it Fluently

- You eat white rice every day of the week and dirty rice on Sunday.
- Your lawn is green on Christmas day.
- You take a shower, but can't dry off.
- You keep Boudain and Gumbo in the freezer.
- You know how to make Okra Gumbo, Jumbalia and Crawfish E'tauffee.
- You drink coffee with Chicory from a demi-tas (a half cup).
- You say "that's so true" or "talk about" when you agree with someone.
- You say non, for no and may yea for yes.
- You prefer Zydeco to any other music.
- You eat breakfast, dinner and supper.
- You call your aunts, Taunt and your uncles Unk.
- You call your Grandparents Mawmon and Papa.
- Your last name is not spelled the way it sounds.
- A part of greeting some one is asking (hows you Mama and them).
- You can pronounce Tchoupitoulas, Thibodeaux, Opelousas, Pouchantrain, Atchafalaya and Natchitoches.
- You pronounce New Orleans, Nawlins.
- In the country there are no street names, so you better know where you're going.

THE DICTIONARY

There are different types of Creole spoken in Louisiana. This is the language spoken in the general area where I was brought up, which is what follows in the pages of this dictionary. The words are taken from the French language, but are different from French, you will recognize some words as French. This is an easy way for the beginner to learn Creole. But remember, nothing is learned without practice and effort. As much as possible the words are spelled the way they sound (which drove my computer crazy).

A unique feature of this dictionary is that, you find the English word that you want to use and next to it you will see the word in Creole. Then, a sentence follows as to how to use it along with an English sentence to interpret it. There is also a CD so that you can hear the sounds of Creole. Our older generation did not have a lot of education or a large vocabulary of words to put in this dictionary, but we feel that it is well worth the effort to include it since is not being passed on to the younger generation and is considered to be a dying language. To my knowledge there is no other dictionary of this type available.

Living Creole and Speaking it Fluently

Bon jour, this is Vivian and this is a dictionary to teach you to speak Creole. The majority of the words are not French, but a compilation of Creole and French words that were used in the general area where I grew up. The words are spelled the way they sound. Most of the time the letter (a) sounds as in star, or (Ah). It can be used for to, at, by, in or for. The regular a will be underlined.

able.....puva, John puva pa travia ojourdwe. John cannot work today.
active.....actif, E son tras actif. They are very active.
address.....address, Ja puva pa trouva l'adress. I could not find the address.
affair.....an affaire, a thing, Set an grond affaire. It's a big celebration.
after.....apre, Apre too sa, e la patie. After all that he has left.
after noon.....apra medi, Tou le jour apre medi e lame macha. He likes to walk every after noon.
again.....oncarr, Ea la ratourni oncarr. He came back again.
age.....igge, Parson coni pa son igge. No one knows his age.
ago.....ton passa, Lon ton passa enava das-anemals etrange ci la tere. Long ago there were strange animals on the land.
all.....tou, Tou la jour say pa la main choze. Every day is not the same thing.
almost.....presqa, Presqa tou le jour e vian acci. Almost every day he comes here.
alone.....sael, John, sa la sael ka arrive. John is the only one who has arrived.
already.....daja, E la dija monge. He has already eaten.
also.....occi, Marie va alla occi. Mary wants to go also.
always.....tolton, E la tolton fain. He is always hungry.
America.....Americaine, E la Americaine. He is American.

angry·····fache, He l<u>a</u> fache. He is angry.
animal·····animal, Set an grand animal. That is a big animal.
answer·····rapon, Rapon moi si vos plait. Please answer me.
apple·····an pomme, An pomme ea bon pour <u>tou</u>a. An apple is good for you.
arm·····le bra, Son bra fa mail. His arm hurts.
around·····<u>a</u>tourd, Ea l<u>a</u> atourd la maison. He is around the house.
arrive·····arriva, Ea l<u>a</u> arriva. He has arrived.
as·····comm, S<u>a</u> pa comm ea de. It is not as he says.
as much,·····oton, S<u>a</u> pa oton que l'ortre. It's not as much as the other.
ask·····monda, Ee la monda ma nom. He asked my name.
aunt·····taunt, La seur d<u>a</u> ma moma s<u>a</u> ma taunt. My mom's sister is my aunt.
automobile·····char, Mon char e<u>a</u> noveau. My car is new.

baby·····b<u>a</u>b<u>a</u>, Cher peti b<u>a</u>b<u>a</u>. Dear little baby.
bad·····movis, E l<u>a</u> movis. He is bad.
ball·····la balle, Allons a la bal. Let's go to the ball.
be·····etra, Pour etra, ou pa pour etra. To be, or not to be.
beautiful·····belle, Ell e<u>a</u> belle. She is beautiful.
become·····viner, Ea va viner gros. He will become large.
bed·····lee, Ea l<u>a</u> couchee dan lee. He is sleeping in bed.
before·····avon, Ea mach avon le othre. He walks before the others.
begin·····commonsa, Ea l<u>a</u> daja commons<u>a</u>. He has already started.
believe·····croi, J<u>a</u> croi pas sa. I don't believe that.

Living Creole and Speaking it Fluently

bell·····cloche, La cloche a sonna ducemon. The bell rang slowly.
belong·····pour, Sa pour Marie. It belongs to Marie.
below·····umba, E la umba la table. He is under the table.
best·····la meyer, E la pri la meyer. He took the best one.
bicycle·····byciclett, El-lem vortre daci la byciclett. He loves to ride the bicycle.
big·····grund, E la des'efon grund. He has grown children.
bird·····ozzo, L'ozzo voture sed pour le verr. The birds fly south for the winter.
birthday·····feit, Oujour'duie sa ma feit. Today is my birthday.
black·····noir, Sa chavre ea noir. Her hair is black.
blue·····bleu, Sa robe ea bleu. Her dress is blue.
blush·····rougir, Sa figure ea rougir. Her face is blushed.
boat·····bato, Moi ja ve an bato deci la rivierr. I saw a boat on the river.
body·····cor, Mon cor ea bien santa macnon. My body is healthy now.
book·····leavre, Ja prata an levre a la bibliotheque. I borrowed a book from the library.
born····· anne, La baba a enna yier a medi. The baby was born yesterday at noon.
borrow·····prata, Ell la prata an leavre avec moi. She borrowed a book from me.
bottle·····bouteie, Ja an boutier de vin. I have a bottle of wine.
box·····boute, E la an boute da soua. He has a shoe box.
boy·····gason, Sa say mon gason. That is my boy.
brave·····brava, Ea la brav. He is brave.
bread·····pain, Jame De bon pain frech. I love good fresh bread.
break·····cassa, Ea la cassa an viere. He broke a glass.
breakfast·····daegena, Sa important pour manga daegena. It is important to eat breakfast.

bridge·····pon, La char a travissa la pon. The car went over the bridge.

bring·····apporta, Ci vou pla, apporta sa a Marie. Please take this to Marie.

brother·····frier, Sa say mon frier. That is my brother.

brown·····brun, Le soua ea brun. The shoes are brown.

brush·····bross, An bross pour brosa le dan. A tooth brush to brush the teeth.

build·····bati, Ja bati an ground mason. I built a big house.

bus·····autobus, Jame pron le auto bus. I like to ride the bus.

but····· main, Ja eta sa Joseph, main e la ta pa la. I went to Joseph's but he was not there.

butter·····bear, Ja-am de bear avec de pain. I like butter with bread.

buy·····ajeta, Ja vula ajata se la. I want to buy that one.

cake·····gato, Ja ame de gato chocolate. I like chocolate cake.

call·····appelle, Appell moi ci vou pla. Please call me.

carry·····porta, Porter an bocke doa. Bring a bucket of water.

cat·····cha, Le shien courir apre la cha. The dogs chase the cat.

cause·····cause, Ja monka mon appointmen a cause da traffic. I missed my appointment because of traffic.

chair·····chaise, La chaise ea comfortable. The chair is comfortable.

change·····chanza, Alons a Lafayette pour fai chanze ton nam. Let's go to Lafayette to change your name.

cheese·····fromage, Sa de fromage Francais. This is French cheese.

child·····onfan, Le onfan a set on. The child is seven years old.

chocolate·····chocolate, Sa de bon-bon chocolate. These are chocolate candies.

church·····eglise, Ja ame allea a l'ehlise la Demashe. I like to go to church on Sundays.

city·····ville, Jim reste dan la vill da Denver. Jim lives in the city of Denver.

class·····clas, Sa la clas da Mesuir Thibodeaux. It's Mr Thibodeaux's class.

clean·····nattoyea, Charlie a bien nattoyea la chomb. Charlie cleaned the room really well.

clock·····pondule, La pondule a daux heir. The clock has two o'clock.

close·····fram, Fram la porta. Close the door.

coffee·····café, Ami vou de café? Would you like some coffee?

cold·····froid, Sa fa froid dan levair. It gets cold in winter.

come·····vienn, Vian aci la semain ke vian. Come here next week.

come back·····revenir, Revenir a ma maison demain. Come back to my house tomorrow.

come down·····desand, Desand da l'arbre. Get down out of the tree.

come in·····untra, Untra dan la maison. Come in to the house.

come up·····monta, Jim va monta l'arbre. Jim will climb up the tree.

correct·····correct, Sa e deia sa correct. What he says is correct.

cost·····cuta, Sa cuta sharre. It costs a lot.

cover·····couverr, Sa sa an jolie cuverre da lei. That is a pretty bed cover.

coward·····capon, Paul ea thro capon pour bata. Paul is too cowardly to fight.

cross·····travesa, E la travesa la chamin. He crossed the street.

cruel·····crull, Sa say crull. That is cruel.

cry·····plarer, Linda a commasa plarer. Linda started to cry.

cup·····tass, Donna moi an tass da café ci vou pla. Give me a cup of coffee please.
cut·····cuppa, Sa ton pour cuppa le zabb. It's time to cut the grass.
curtain·····redeau, An redeau va deci an fannit. A curtain goes on a window.

dance·····danca, E lam danca. He likes to dance.
daughter·····fille, Catherine sa ma fille. Catherine is my daughter.
dear·····chare, Oie mon chare. Yes my dear.
decide·····decda, E la decda pour son aller. He decided to leave.
defend·····defond, E la bazoin un avoca pours defond. He needs a lawyer to defend him.
delicious·····delicea, La gato ea delicea. The cake is delicious.
die—mourie, Tool monde va mourie. All people will die.
difficult·····diffecile, Sa diffecile pour fait la lesson. The lessons are difficult.
dirty·····salle, Sa souia ea sall. His shoes are dirty.
do·····faire, Ja-va faire sa pour toua. I will do this for you.
doctor·····doctair, Ja bazoin allar a doctair. I need to go to the doctor.
dog·····chien, La chien curre viet. The dog ran fast.
dollar·····dolla, an piace, La borrette a coutte an piace. The borrette cost one dollar.
door·····porrta, Frama la porrta. Close the door.
down·····umba, Umba la maison sa boucou noir. Under the house it is very dark.

downtown·····un ville, Sh'ame pron la bus un ville. I like to ride the bus down town.
dozen·····douzenne, Ja an douzenne des euf. I have one dozen eggs.
dress·····robe, Pam a an joli robe rouge. Pam has a pretty red dress.
dressed·····drassa, Joe ea dressa tou dan noir. Joe is dressed all in black.
drink·····boire, E va boire an tass da café. He will drink a cup of coffee.
dry·····sec, La capo ea to sec. The coat is all dry.
don't·····faix, Faix pa sa. Don't do that.

each·····chak, A chak son maim. To each his own.
early·····bonnair, Sa thro bonnair pou lava. It is too early to get up.
earn·····gonaia, E la gonaia sonn argent. He earned his money.
easy·····facille, Sa ci facille pour acrit an letter. It is very easy to write a letter.
eat·····monge, Sa important pour mange dagana. It is important to eat breakfast.
egg·····euf, Ja monge deaux seuf pour dagana. I ate two eggs for breakfast.
eight·····wheat, Sa la wheatem foir. It is the eighth time.
eighty·····quatra ven, Ja conta quatra van dollas. I counted eighty dollars.
eleveter·····acentier, Ja entra la acentier. I got on the elevator.
eleven·····onze, Sa onze heure. It is eleven o'clock.
empty·····veid, La boka ea veid. The bucket is empty.

enemy·····enemie, S<u>a</u> pa bon avoir d<u>as</u> enemie. It is not good to have enemies.

English·····englase, J<u>a</u> pal bien Englase d<u>a</u>y foi. I speak English well some times.

enough·····assez, S<u>a</u> assez d<u>a</u> monge. That's enough food.

enter·····entra, S<u>a</u> defecil pour entr<u>a</u> la cenema d<u>a</u> foir. Some times it's hard to get in the movies.

error·····errare, S<u>a</u> un errare pour pons<u>a</u> toul monde e<u>a</u> genteel. It's an error to believe that all people are kind.

especially·····espri, J<u>a</u> veni espri pour t'woa. I came especially to see you.

evening·····soir, L<u>as</u> etoile e<u>a</u> brilliant le soir. The stars are bright at night.

every·····too, Too le jour ja aller dan village. Every day I go to town.

everybody·····to kalkan, Tou-le monde danc<u>a</u>. Every body is dancing.

everywhere·····topato, El voyager to pa to. She travels everywhere.

examination·····examination, La doctair va f<u>a</u>ir an examination deci moi. The doctor will examine me.

expensive·····cher, La robe a couta cher. The dress was expensive.

explain·····expleka, Expleka moi la convasasion. Explain the conversation to me.

eyes·····le-zyeau, E ma fait d<u>a</u> zyeau doux. He made sweet eyes at me.

face·····figure, E la brasser ma figure. He kissed my face.

fall·····tomba, El a tomb<u>a</u> deci sa figure. She fell on her face.

Living Creole and Speaking it Fluently

family·····famille, Moi ja un grand famille. I have a large family.
famous·····celebra, E la an person celebra. He is a famous person.
far·····loin, E rest loin da moi. He lives far from me.
fat·····gras, He la gras. He is fat.
father·····pere, Mon pere ea faut. My father is strong.
feather·····plumm, Son chapeau ea fait avec da plumm. Her hat is made with feathers.
few····· pae, An pae de monde a keta bonair. A few people left early.
fewer·····moins, Moins que cinquante a resta. Fewer than fifty stayed.
fill·····rempli, Rempli le verre avec de vin. Fill the glasses with wine.
find·····trouver, Nou pa pa trouva Fido. We cannot find Fido.
fine·····beau, belle, El ea beau. She is fine.
finish·····fenne, E la fenne monage. He has finished eating.
fire·····fea, La fea a brillia sa main. The fire burned his hand.
first·····premier, Sa ta an premier cenema. It was a first movie.
fish·····poisson, El am pasha pour de poisson. He loves to fish.
flower····· fleur, E la voier un bouque da fleur rouge. He sent a bouquet of red flowers.
follow·····suive, E ma suev dan son char. He followed me in his car.
foolish·····fou, E la ci fou. He is so foolish.
foot·····peae, Sa peae a pa-da souia. He has no shoes on his feet.
forget·····obelia, Moi ja obelia ma lesence. I forgot my license.
free·····lebre, Moi ja lebre ea majaur. I am free and liberated.
French····· Francais, E pall bien Francais. He speaks French very well .
fresh·····frache, De pain freshe ea ci bon. Fresh bread is so good.

Vivian Malveaux

Friday·····Vandedrie, ja va aller trivi<u>a</u>. I go to work on Friday.
fruit·····fre, D<u>a</u> fre ea ci bon pour toua. Fruit is very good for you.
full·····plein, Son estoma e<u>a</u> plen. His stomach is full.

game·····juer, La petit ap<u>a</u> juer. The children are playing.
garden·····jardin, La gardin <u>a</u> plen-de fleur. The garden is full of flowers.
gentle·····gentelle, He l<u>a</u> ci gentelle. He is so gentle.
gentlemen····· le mesieur, Le mesieur <u>a</u> bien abi<u>a</u>. The gentlemen are well dressed.
gently·····doucemon, El pal doucemon. He speaks gently.
get up·····lava, Sa tro bonair pour lav<u>a</u>. Its too early to get up.
gift·····cadeau, E ma donn<u>a</u> <u>a</u>n jolie cadeau. He gave me a pretty gift.
girl·····jaun fiell, <u>A</u>n jaun fiell a pass<u>a</u> la porte. A young girl passed by the door.
give·····donna, E la donna <u>a</u>n packa. He gives her a package.
glad·····conton, Ell <u>a</u> ci conton. She is so glad.
glass·····verre, J<u>a</u> be<u>a</u> <u>a</u>n varre de vin. I drank a glass of wine.
glove·····gan, Ell la perde sa gan. She lost her glove.
go·····aller, Aller a la boutique. Go to the store.
go away·····parti, E l<u>a</u> parti laba. He is going there.
go back·····retunna, E va retunna damian. He will return tomorrow.
go down·····decend<u>a</u>, La garson a desonde l'abre. The boy decended the tree.
going·····parti, E l<u>a</u> parti laba. He has gone over there.
go out····· sorte, E la sorte d<u>a</u> la porta. He went out the door.

go up·····monta, L'abra ea thro hout pour monta. The tree is too high to climb.
good·····bon, Marie a bon emmer. Marie has good humor.
good bye·····a Dea. Go with God.
good day·····Bon Jour.
grand father·····gron- pere, Ja-me ton mon gron-pere. I love my grand father so much.
grass·····zabe, La zabe ea verrt. The grass is green.

hair·····cheva, Mai cheva ea gra. My hair is gray.
half·····demi, moche, Ja monga la moche da denna. I ate half of my dinner.
hand·····main, Largent ea dan mia main. The money is in my hand.
hankerchief·····mouchoir, Ja an mouchoir dan ma poche. I have a handkerchief in my pocket.
handsome·····beau, Mon homme ea beau. My man is handsome.
happy·····heureu, Ea la toul ton heureu. He is always happy.
hard·····deau, E son an vie deau. They have a hard life.
have·····avoir, Saya avoir pasance avec el. Try to have patience with her.
head·····tete, Ell a mal da tete. She has a headache.
hear·····entendre, E la tondre qui ell a dee. He heard what she said.
heart·····coeur, Oheie mon coeur fai mal. Oooooh my heart aches.
heavy·····lourd, E la porta an lourd deur. He carried a heavy load.

help·····aide, E ma aide. He helped me.
here·····aci, Vien aci a moi toot suite. Hurry and come to me.
high·····haut, E la asenda haut. He went up high.
hold·····chomb, Chomb la main de la peti. Hold the child's hand.
home·····maison, Moi sha an maison grand. I have a big house.
hope·····espere, E la espere dan Deau. He has hope in God.
horse·····cheval, E mettre le chavel dan la cour. He put the horse in the yard.
hot·····chod, Sa fait thro shod dan la Louisiana. It is too hot in Louisiana.
hotel·····otel, Ja rasta dan an otel. I stayed in a hotel.
hour·····l'heur, A qul heur say? What time is it?
how·····combien, Combien da monde ea dan la chomb? How many people are in the room?
hundred·····soan, Ja paya soan piace pour la robe. I paid one hundred dollars for the dress.
hurry·····depache, Depacha avec la triver. Hurry with the work.
hurt·····faire mal, Mon doa faire mal. My back hurts.
husband·····mari, Son marie ea mashon. Her husband is mean.

immediately·····tout-d-suite, Veint tout-d-suite. Come here immediately.
intelligent·····intelligen, Le petit son tres intelligen. The children are very intelligent.
invite·····invita, Ja inveta Marie pour vanair a ma maison. I invited Marie to my house.

January·····Janvier sa la premier morr dan lunay. January is the first month of the year
jewels·····beju, Ja boucou da beju. I have lots of jewelry

keep·····gardir, E va gardir se la. He will keep that one.
key·····clef, Ja perdi la clef. I lost the key.
kind·····gentille, El ea gentille. She is kind.
King·····le roi, Le roi a visita les Atas Unis. The King visited the United States.
kitchen·····cuisine, Moi ja an grond cuisine. I have a large kitchen.
knife·····couteau, La couteau a seir la table. The knife is on the table.
know·····savoir, Savoir faire. He acts knowingly, he's been around.
know·····cona, Ja cona la lang da Creole. I know the Creole language.

lady·····dame, La dame ea jolie. The lady is pretty.
lake, la lac, L'eau dan la lac ea ba. The water in the lake is low.
language·····laung, Ja am aprond an laung differant. I like to learn different languages.
large·····grand, El ea an grand femme. She is a big woman.
last·····dannier, E son tujure le dannier pour entra. They are always the last to enter.

late·····tard, S<u>a</u> pasque e l<u>a</u> toujure tard. It's because he is always late.
laugh·····rire, El-<u>a</u>m boucou rire. She likes to laugh.
lawyer·····avoca, E la biozion un avoco. He needs a lawyer.
lazy·····paressea, El l<u>a</u> tres paressea. She is very lazy.
learn·····aprenda, Estud<u>a</u> duer pour apron la lesson. Study hard to learn the lesson.
leave·····partir, laisser, Laisser f<u>a</u>ire. Leave it alone.
left·····gauche, J<u>a</u> ecrie avec ma main gauche. I wrote with my left hand.
lend·····preter, J<u>a</u> preter sonn piace avec John. I borrowed one hundred dollars from John.
less·····moins, Moins de monde va a l'eglase aujourd'hui. Fewer people go to church today.
lesson·····lesson, J<u>a</u> appre <u>a</u>n lesson. I learned a lesson.
letter·····lettre, J<u>a</u> acre <u>a</u>n lettre a ma mere. I wrote a letter to my mother.
let us·····lasa, Las<u>a</u> nous alle<u>a</u> a restaurant pour monge. Let us go to the restaurant to eat.
lie down·····coucher, Vien coucher avec moi. Come sleep with me.
life·····vie, Sa la vie. That's life.
lift·····lavea, Lave<u>a</u> ton voi a chanta. Lift up your voice in song.
light····· lemiera, Lemiera la lamp pour <u>a</u>cre ton letre. Light the lamp to write your letter.
like·····aimer, J<u>a</u>'aim aller a cenema. I like to go to the movies.
listen·····accuter, <u>A</u>ccuter la sashon, s<u>a</u> ci belle. Listen to the beautiful song.
little·····petit, pe, S<u>a</u> <u>a</u>n pe thro tard. It's a little too late.
live·····reste, E reste don village. He lives in the city.
lively·····vevant, El e<u>a</u> tres vevant. She is very lively.
long····· lontemps, Lontemps pass<u>a</u>, presque tou nu vie<u>a</u> monde parl<u>a</u> Creole. A long time ago most of our older people spoke Creole.

look at·····regardaer, Regardaer l<u>a</u> belle maison. Look at the beautiful house.
look for·····charcher, Charcher la fame. Look for the woman.
lose·····perdre, E va perdre sa maison. He will lose his house.
loud·····haut, La musick e<u>a</u> thro haut. The music is too loud.
low·····basse, Basse la musick se vou pla. Lower the music, please.
love·····lamare, J'amm la petet baby. I love the little baby.

man·····homme, L'homme a venir a sa fame. The man came back to his wife.
many·····boucou, E la boucou das'ufon. He has many children.
market·····le marche, Too la famille va aller a la marche. The whole family is going to the market.
maybe·····paetet, Paetet ea von too reviner onsumb. Maybe they will come back together.
meal·····an repas, J<u>a</u> ea <u>a</u>n repas a la restaurant. I had a meal at the restaurant.
meat·····vien, J<u>a</u> e <u>a</u>n samage d<u>a</u> vien poule. I had a chicken sandwich.
mean·····mechant, E l<u>a</u> mechant. He is mean.
middle·····milieu, Dan la milieu da jour. In the middle of the day.
midnight·····minuit, Minuit a soir s<u>a</u> la fet da novella ana. At midnight it will be New Year.
milk·····lait, An bon tass de lait sho. A good hot cup of milk.
million·····million, <u>A</u>n million, s<u>a</u> too. Only one million.
minute·····minute, <u>A</u>n minute ci vou plas. One minute please.
Miss····· madamoiselle, Madamoiselle Comeaux e<u>a</u> pa marrie. Miss Comeaux is not married.

Vivian Malveaux

mistake·····erreur, E la fait an erreur. He made a mistake.
Monday·····Laundi, E va retunner Laundi. He will return on Monday
money·····l'argent, E la boucu da argent. He has a lot of money.
month·····mois, Dan la mois da Julet sa ma fet. My birthday is in July.
moon·····la lune, La lune ea plien. The moon is full.
more·····plus, Plus de pain ci vous pla. More bread, if you please.
morning·····matin, El emer marche le matin. She likes to walk in the morning.
mother·····mere, Ma mere ea tres gentile. My mother is very kind.
movie·····cenema, Ja vie Robere a la cenema. I saw Robert at the movie.
Mr.·····meseur, Meseur Thibodeaux ea malade. Mr. Thibodeaux is sick.
Mrs.·····Madam, Madam Thibodeaux a pour la sonyea. Mrs. Thibodeaux has to take care of him.
much·····beaucoup, E la beaucoup da medicin. He has a lot of medicine.

name·····nom, Mon nam sa Robere. My name is Robert.
need·····avoir bizoin, El avoir bizoin an doctair. He needs a doctor.
neighbor·····voisin, Ma voisin pal thro. My neighbor talks too much.
nephew·····neveu, Mon neveu ea noma Daniel. My nephew's name is Daniel.
never·····jamais, Maan jamais. Well I never.
new·····nouvea, El a an nouvea chapeau. She has a new hat.

Living Creole and Speaking it Fluently

next·····ensuite, Moi ja ensuite mon frer. I am next to my brother.
night·····nuit, Le nuit son long dan lever. The nights are long in winter.
ninth·····neuvieme, Say la nehvieme fouir sa arrive. It's the ninth time that happened.
noon·····medi, Ja am monge a medi. I like to eat at noon.
nose·····na, Son na eta rouge. His nose was red.
notebook·····cayeas, Ja bizoin an cayea. I need a notebook.
now·····maintenant, Maintenant ja vouler dolmi. Now I want to sleep.

of·····da, Sa vaine da moi. It came from me.
offer·····offrir, El a offrir de café. She offered some coffee.
often·····souvent, Sa pa souvent e va laba. It's not often that he goes there.
old·····vieux, Sa an village ka vieux. It's an old town.
open·····ouvrir, Ouvrir la porte. Open the door.
opportunity·····l'occasion, Sa an occasion pour fair de bien. It's an opportunity to do good.
other·····autre, An autre famm apa marche. Another woman is walking.
overcoat·····capo, Son capo a noir. His coat is black.

package·····packet, E la an grand packet. He has a big package.
paper·····papier, Acrie de ci le papier. Write on the papers.

Vivian Malveaux

park·····parc, Ja an lecense pour la pac. I have a licence for the park.
pass·····passa, Ja passa devont ta porta. I passed in front of your door.
pay·····paya, Ja paya pour le souia. I paid for the shoes.
pencil·····crayon, La petit a perdi son crayon. The child lost her pencil.
perhaps·····patete, Patete nous va sil voir a demain. Perhaps we will see you tomorrow.
pick up·····ramasser, Ramasser la baba. Pickup the baby.
picture·····polture, Sa an bon polture. That's a good picture.
piece·····morceau, Jus an peti morceau. Just a small piece.
plane·····le avion, Ja pre le avion pour aller a Parie. I took the plane to go to Paris.
play·····jouer, Le petit lama jouer. The children love to play.
pleasant·····agreable, E la agreable pour too quil chose. He is agreeable about everything.
please·····ci vous'plait, Donna moi da fri se vous pla. Please give me some fruit.
pocket·····la poche, El a d'argent dan sa poche. He has money in his pocket.
polite·····poli, El ea poli. She is polite.
poor·····pauvre, E na boucou da pauvre monde dan La Novelle Orleans. There are a lot of poor people in New Orleans.
pound·····levre, Sa eta cinc levre. It was five pounds.
prefer·····preferea, Marie preferea l'ortre. Marie prefers the other one.
prepare·····preparer, E vas preparer pour sa marriage. He will prepare for his marriage.
present····· la cadeau, El a boucou da cadeau. She has a lot of presents.
pretty·····jolie, El ea joli. She is pretty.
price·····la pri, La pri da too quil chose coute shar. Everything costs too much.

Living Creole and Speaking it Fluently

princess·····princesse, La princesse ea tras belle. The princess is very beautiful.
promise·····prometre, El a prometre la marriage. She made a promise to marry.
proud·····fier, E l<u>a</u> tras fier. He is very proud.
punish·····penir, E devire etra penir. He should be punished.
put·····mettre, Ou pour mettre? Where should I put it?

quarter·····quart, Mon argent e<u>a</u> too dan l<u>a</u> quart. All my money is in quarters.
queen·····la reine, La reine apra venier a Americ. The queen is coming to America.
question·····question, J<u>a</u> un question pour vou. I have a question for you.
quickly·····vite, Vien vite. Come here fast.

rain·····pluie, Sa pluie a souir. It's raining tonight.
rapidly·····rapidement, Ea travia rapidement. He works rapidly.
raise·····lever, Lever la monche. Raise the arm.
read·····lire, Marie apre lire <u>a</u>n levre. Marie is reading a book.
ready·····praparie, Praparie pour aller a la maison. Get ready to go home.
really·····veramon, J<u>a</u> veramon seur. I am really sure.
receive·····receviea, Moi ja receviea an packa. I received a package.

red·····rouge, Sa figure e<u>a</u> rouge. His face is red.
reflect·····poncer, J<u>a</u> poncer sa pour an long ton. I reflected on that for a long time.
remain·····rester, E va rester laba. He will stay over there.
restaurant·····resturan, J<u>a</u> <u>a</u>m monge a la resturan Creole. I like to eat at a Creole restaurant
return·····revenair, E va reven<u>ai</u>r damain. He will return tomorrow.
rich·····riche, E son riche. They are rich.
ring·····soner, Soner la clouch. Ring the bell.
road·····chemin, J<u>a</u> pre la premier chemin j<u>a</u> arrive. I took the first street I came to.
round·····rond, E l<u>a</u> rond com <u>a</u>n bak<u>a</u>. He is as round as a bucket.
rug·····tapis, La tapis a bizoin netoi<u>a</u>. The rug needs cleaning.
run·····courir, E la courie dan la chemin. He ran into the street.

salt·····sal, <u>A</u>n bouite d<u>a</u> sal. A box of salt.
Saturday·····Semedi, La Semedi j<u>a</u> <u>a</u>m coucher tard. I like to sleep late on Saturday.
say·····dire, He la dire la velati<u>a</u>. He told the truth.
school·····l'acole, Las ufants allier a l'acole. The children go to school.
season·····sason, La sason d<u>a</u> levaire e<u>a</u> froid dan Denver. It is cold in Denver in the winter time.
seated·····assi, Resti assi, ci vou si pl<u>a</u>. Remain seated please.
second·····deuxieme, Sa la deauxieme foir sa arriv. It's the second time that's happened.
see·····voir, Aallons voir le etoiles s<u>a</u> soui. Let's go look at the stars tonight.

seize·····seisir, E la seisir le pap*a*i dan ma chomb. He seized the papers from my room.
seldom·····rearment, S*a* rearment j*a* va a sa maison. It's rare that I go to her house.
sell·····vendre, J*a* vendre d*a* legumes. I sold some vegetables.
send·····envoyer, Envoyer *a*n bouque da fleur a Marie. Send a bouquet of flowers to Marie.
September·····Septame, Le feuille e*a* belle dan Septame, The leaves are beautiful in September.
serious·····serieux, Marie e*a* John son serieux. Marie and John are serious.
serve·····servier, E la servier da Hors-d-oevrire ea de vin. He served snacks and wine.
several·····plusieurs, E la plusieurs da-homme quie v*a* de cafe. Several men want coffee.
shame·····honte, Sa fait honte. It is a shame.
shine·····brilier, Le sou*a* a John e*a* brilion. John's shoes are shiny.
shoe·····soua, John a da gro sou*a*. John has big shoes.
short·····cour, *A*n petit famm e*a* cour. A little woman is short.
sick·····malade, E l*a* malade. He is sick.
silent·····mute, Mettre la TV mute ci vous pla. Please put the TV on mute.
silk·····soie, An robe d*a* soie cutta shar. A silk dress costs a lot.
silly·····bukie, Hey, s*a* bukie. Hey, there's silly.
sing·····chanter, Le jeun monde l*a*me chanter. The young people like to sing.
Sir·····messieur, Messieur Como a *a*n belle maison. Mr. Como has a beautiful house.
sister·····seur, Say sa mon seur. That is my sister.
sixteen·····seize, El la seize *a*n. She is sixteen years old.
sixty·····soixante, Son mere a soixante. Her mother is sixty.
sky·····ciel, La ciel e*a* ble. The sky is blue.
sleep·····dolmer, E l*a* pa p*a* dolme. He is not sleeping.

slow·····dusemon, Va dusemon. Go slow.
small·····petit, La efant ea petit. The child is small.
snow·····neiger, Sa apra neiger dan le mountan. It is snowing in the mountains.
so·····allour, Allour, ja fenne paller avec toa. So, I am finished talking to you.
so much·····ton, Sa ci ton da orange. That's a lot of oranges.
someone·····quelque, Ena quelque a la porte. There is someone at the door.
something·····quelque chose, E la quelque chose dan se main. He has something in his hands.
sometimes·····queque foi, Queque foi ja am aller a la pac. Sometimes I like to go to the park.
son·····fis, Mon fis va alley pour an doctair. My son is going for a doctor.
song·····chanson, Sa an bon chanson. That is a good song.
soon·····bienton, E va arriver a bienton. He will arrive soon.
south·····sud, Le ozzo voutture a la sud dan lever. Birds fly south for the winter.
speak·····paller, E puva pa paller dan publique. He could not speak in public.
spend·····passer, Nous a passer an bon ton a la Zydeco. We passed a good time at the Zydeco.
spring·····prenton, Prenton sa la maier ton dan lana. Spring time is the best time of the year.
stay·····resta, E va resta la. He will stay there.
store·····magasin, E vons aller a magasin. They will go to the store.
stop·····ahretta, Ci vou pla, ahretta parla. Please stop talking.
strange·····etrange, Paller pa avec das etrange. Don't talk to strangers.
street·····chimin, Pron la chimin a la lemiaire. Take the street at the light.
strong·····far, E la ci far. He is so strong.

study·····etudier, E l<u>a</u> etudier san lesson. He studied his lesson.
suddenly·····tou-dan-cou, Too-dan-cou e l<u>a</u> partie. Suddenly he was gone.
sugar·····secre, La secre e<u>a</u> si la tabla. The sugar is on the table.
summer·····l'ete, Sa fait shod dan l'ete. It is hot in summer.
Sunday·····Demoche, J<u>a</u> va a l'eglase le Demoche. I go to church on Sunday.
sure·····sur, J<u>a</u> seur s<u>a</u> pa la mem famm. I am sure it is not the same woman.
sweet·····doux, La vin ea tro doux. The wine is too sweet.

table·····tabla, Dinna ea sur la tabla. Dinner is on the table.
take·····pranda, E va pranda too qil choze. He will take every thing.
take off·····oter, Oter le gan. Take off the gloves.
tall·····grand, Too la frai son grand. All the brothers are tall.
tea·····tha, J<u>a</u> toul ton boi de tha. I always drink tea.
tell—dire, J<u>a</u> va dire la velita. I will tell the truth.
than·····que, D'orta que moi parson va pa. No one is going other than me.
then·····alors, Alors sa pa moi que plurer. Then it's not me that cries.
there·····la, Wa la. Look there.
thick·····apy, S<u>a</u>et an soup <u>a</u>py. This is a thick soup.
thing·····chose, Too la jour s<u>a</u> pa la mamm chose. Every day is not the same thing.
think·····penser, J<u>a</u> ponsie too la journa pour tou. I taught of you all day long.
thirteen·····treize, La garson a triez un. The boy is thirteen years old.

thirty·····tronta, Son papa a tronta neif. His father is thirty nine.
thousand·····mille, E la mille peise. He has a thousand dollars.
throw·····jeter, Jeter la ploat. Throw the ball.
Thursday·····Jeudi, Jeudi sa an joir pour travira. Thursday is a working day.
tie·····cravat, Sa cravat ea soie. His tie is silk
tired·····fatigue, Ja tras fatigue. I am very tired.
today·····oujourduie, Oujourduie sa Laundi. Today is Monday.
together·····unsam, La famil rest unsam. The family stays together.
tomorrow·····demain, Eshca demain. Until tomorrow.
tonight·····asouir, Patet ja va resta eshca asoir. Maybe I'll stay until tonight.
too·····tho, Sha tro da leavre. I have too many books.
tooth·····dan, Sha mal a dan. I have a tooth ache.
train·····train, Ja am voyage pa tramway. I love to travel by streetcar.
translate·····tradure, Tradure pour moi la langue Creole a Anglais. Translate for me from Creole to English.
travel·····voyager, Ja vuloua voyager dan France. I would like to travel to France.
tree·····l'erbe, L'erbe ea tras grand. The tree is very tall.
trip·····voyage, John va apron an voyage. John is going to take a trip.
true·····vrai, Sa e dee sa vrai. What he says is true.
truth·····vileta, Sa la vileta. It is true.
try on·····issayer, E va issayer la suit. He will try on the suit.
Tuesday·····Mardi, Mardi Gras sa boucou bon ton. Fat Tuesday is a good time.
turn·····touna, Ja tourna dan la chimin. I turned around in the street.
twelve·····douze, A douze heir ja va mange. At twelve noon I want to eat lunch.
twenty·····vant, E le vant deaux aun. He is twenty two years old.

ugly·····velin, Ja truve sa an velin chin. I find that is an ugly dog.
umbrella·····parisall, E la pre son parisall o joudi. He took his umbrella today.
uncle·····nock, E na an chanson qe sa pell nock Elair. There is a song called uncle Elair.
under·····umba, L'enfant a casha umba la table. The children hid under the table.
understand·····compran, Ja compran pa la-Italian. I don't understand Italian.
unhappy·····malheureux, E le malheureux. He is misarable.
United States·····E'tats-Unis, An taa de monde va venier a les E'tats-Unis. A lot of people want to come to the United States.
upstairs·····on hau, Allon on hau a ma chamb. Let's go upstairs to my room.
use·····usa, Ja bazion usa la coutoe pour cupa la vian. I need to use the knife to cut the meat.
vacation·····vacazion, Sa ton pour en vacazion. It is time for a vacation.
vegetable·····legume, De legume ea bon pour toar. Vegetables are good for you.
very·····tres, El ea tras polit. She is very polite.
visit·····visite, E ma visite long ton passa. He visited me a long time ago.
voice·····voi, La voi da la feil ea hou. The girl's voice is high.

wait·····espaire, Espaire pour moi. Wait for me.
waiter·····garson, Garson, an vair de vin se vou-plai. Waiter, a glass of wine please.
walk·····macha, E va mache too le jour. He walks every day.

Vivian Malveaux

wall·····mur, E la jat<u>a</u> cont la mur. He threw it against the wall.
want·····voudra, J<u>a</u> voudra woir Marie oncarr. I want to see Marie again.
war·····garre, La garre e<u>a</u> miserable, ea terrible. The war is miserable and terrible.
warm·····cho, J<u>a</u> <u>a</u>m pas con sa fei cho. I hate it when it's hot.
wash·····lava, Lav<u>a</u> le vessel. Wash the dishes.
watch·····gada, J<u>a</u> pour gad<u>a</u> le shodier. I have to watch the pots.
water·····l'eau, J<u>a</u> pouva boire an varre d<u>a</u>-eau. I could drink a glass of water.
weak·····feab, E l<u>a</u> feab, pas qua e l<u>a</u> malade. He is weak because he's sick.
Wednesday·····Macredi, J<u>a</u> v<u>a</u> aller Macredi ke vien. I will go next Wednesday.
week·····semain, La samain qe vien. This week coming.
well·····bien, E l<u>a</u> pa malade ea l<u>a</u> bien. He is not sick, he is well.
what·····qe, Qe s<u>a</u> te pall pour? What are you talking about?
which·····quel, Quel s<u>a</u> vous <u>a</u>m? Which one do you love?
white·····blonch, J<u>a</u> un tant qe nam<u>a</u> Blonch. I have an aunt named Blonch.
who·····qe, Qe s<u>a</u> ke vien? Who is coming?
wicked·····machan, E na da chien q<u>a</u> machan. Those are some very mean dogs.
wide·····gro, S<u>a</u> ton <u>a</u>n gro maison. It is such wide house.
wife·····femme, Sa s<u>a</u> ma femme. That is my wife.
win·····gannai, Marie a gannai la pre. Marie won the prize.
window·····fannite, Ovairre la fannite. Open the window.
wine····· vin, De vin va bien avec de mang<u>a</u>. Wine goes great with food.
winter·····levar, Sa fra dan levar. It is cold in winter.
wish·····desirer, Sa mon desirer pour aller a Parie. It is my desire to go to Paris.

Living Creole and Speaking it Fluently

with·····avec, Ma neis va vener avec moi. My niece will come with me.
without·····sans, Sans le passport nu pov<u>a</u> pa alle<u>a</u> a Parie. Without a passport we cannot go to Paris.
wood·····boi, John reste acouta l<u>a</u> boi. John lives near the woods.
work·····travailler, E va travailler too la jour. He goes to work every day.
world·····monde, Tool monde ea diffeant. All people are different.
write·····acrie, <u>A</u>crie moi un lettra ci vou pla. Write me a letter please.

year·····lana, Lana passa seta <u>a</u>n movis anne. Last year was a bad year.
yellow·····jaune, Jaune s<u>a</u> pa an bon collere pur moi. Yellow is not a good color for me.
yesterday·····yeare, Yeare e ma conta son problem. Yesterday he told me his problem.
yet·····pa oncurr, E son pa la oncurr. They are not there yet.
young·····jeune, La jeune file a <u>a</u>da sa moman. The young girl helped her mother.

Zydeco·····la musick, la donce

LaVergne, TN USA
30 September 2009
159383LV00001B/46/P